Navigating our

NON

LINEAR

world

A Journey Towards Digital Renaissance By
Adopting The DeSIRe Framework

AMIT ADARKAR

STARDOM BOOKS

www.StardomBooks.com

STARDOM BOOKS, LLC

112, Bordeaux Ct,

Coppell, TX 75019

FIRST EDITION DECEMBER 2023

STARDOM BOOKS

A Division of Stardom Alliance
112, Bordeaux Ct,
Coppell, TX 75019
www.stardombooks.com

Stardom Books, United States
Stardom Books, India
The author and publishers have made all reasonable
efforts to contact copyright-holders for permission,
and apologize for any omissions or errors in the form
of credits given. Corrections may be made to future
editions.

Navigating our **Nonlinear** *world:*
Amit Adarkar

p. 136
cm. 13.5 X 21.5

Category: Technology and Engineering / General

ISBN: 978-1-957456-34-8

DEDICATION

I would like to dedicate this book to my late
parents, Supriya and Sudhakar Adarkar. While
they may not be here to hold a copy of this book,
I carry their blessings with me. A heartfelt thank
you to *Aai* and *Baba* for instilling in me the love
of reading.

CONTENTS

ACKNOWLEDGEMENTS

The concept for this book sprouted during a lively family dinner conversation in early 2023, with my wife, Dr. Shilpa, and my son, Saujas. I found myself passionately discussing technology, and their spontaneous suggestion was, "Why don't you write a book about it?" While I'm an avid blogger and my profession involves a lot of talking, the idea of writing a book had never crossed my mind. But that seed took root, and I decided to dive in.

I am immensely grateful to Shilpa for always keeping me grounded and being my unwavering support system. She has been my confidante, mentor, and guide for decades. Without her constant encouragement, support, and valuable feedback, this book would not have come to fruition.

Saujas, your balanced perspective has been invaluable. I admire your maturity and wisdom, which often surpasses my own when I was your age.

I extend my gratitude to my sister, Ashwini, who was my reading companion during our formative years as we devoured books together.

A heartfelt thank you to both the Adarkar and Desai families for their unwavering support.

I would also like to express my appreciation to my friend and ex-colleague, Vijay Raj, for graciously contributing the foreword to this book.

Lastly, my sincere thanks go out to the Stardom team—Sthitodhi, Priyadarshini, Rekha, and Ranjitha—for their patience in dealing with me and assisting me throughout this remarkable journey.

FOREWORD

I am excited to write this introduction about a topic I care deeply about—technology.

Technology refers to all the gadgets, machines, and digital tools we use in our daily lives to make things easier. I believe in the incredible power of technology; it can bring us many advantages, and it's changing very quickly.

Amit reached out to me about his book "**Nonlinear**," and I was naturally thrilled and curious. Amit and I have known each other for many years; we have been coworkers and business partners for over twenty years. We both share a strong belief in technology's power and the importance of using it responsibly.

This book takes us on a journey through the history of technology, from a straightforward, physical world to today's complex digital world. Most importantly, the book explains how technology affects us, the people. You will also learn how Generative Artificial Intelligence might lead to a Digital Renaissance, an exciting time for technology.

Lastly, the book introduces the "DeSIRe" framework, a helpful guide to making the most out of today's technology. As I write this introduction, I recognize that the modern digital world can be overwhelming for many of us.

This book provides some practical and effective tips that you can easily use. I am confident the book will bring value to every reader. I wish you all the best in your reading journey. Enjoy the book!

Vijay Raj,

Head of CMI, Unilever.

INTRODUCTION

The word technology comes from the Greek word *"techne,"* which means art or craft. We have come a long way since then. Today, technology means much more than art or craft. The Oxford Dictionary defines technology as "The application of scientific knowledge for practical purposes." In the simplest sense, technology is the practical application of scientific knowledge to solve problems and improve human welfare. There are two characteristics of technology embedded into this definition. Firstly, it is about applying existing knowledge— not just knowing but also applying it when needed. Secondly, there needs to be a practical purpose for using the application that serves humanity.

Google Books Ngram Viewer says that the word 'technology' started growing rapidly in the late 1960s and peaked around 1990, when 'internet' started dominating the mentions in the published domain. But the reality is that humankind has always deployed technology in various forms throughout our history. Some of the most remarkable illustrations of technology - the printing press, electricity, penicillin, semiconductor electronics, optical lenses, and internal combustion engines have brought about immense progress. Modern-day technology plays a massive role in the betterment of human life. Over the past two to three decades, computers have become an integral part of our lives.

We cannot imagine our daily lives without smartphones, the internet, and social media. We use technology to accomplish several tasks in our daily lives. Digitalization has become such a crucial part of our lives that it is impossible to imagine a life without being surrounded by digital technology. We use technology at work for communication, transportation, entertainment, and education. Modern-day healthcare uses technology extensively. Technology has become like our everyday buddy, helping us with many things, like talking to friends on our phones, learning new stuff on the computer, and even staying healthy with technology in medicine. So, it is safe to say that in today's world, technology is a big part of how we live, work, and have fun, and it's hard to picture life without it.

Whenever technology is utilized ethically and responsibly, it benefits humans, but history has proved that the abuse of technology has led to disaster. Throughout history, examples show how using technology in harmful or irresponsible ways has caused big problems. For instance, in our everyday lives, when we misuse technology, like using our phones too much or spreading false information online, it can create problems in our relationships and society. But that is not the only way technology can harm humankind. Consider the powerful weapons that were developed with technology that has been a product of research for years, like bombs and missiles used in wars, leading to lots of destruction and suffering. Also, using technology to produce products meant to make human life easier, such as electricity from coal-fired power plants, ultimately harms the environment, leading to disasters like climate change and natural disasters.

Nonetheless, when someone mentions the word "Technology," most people immediately see images of devices such as computers, smartphones, or equipment such as aeronautics, aviation, or self-driving cars. However, technology goes back millennia to the Stone Age when our ancestors discovered that sharpened stone could be used as an axe to hunt animals.

Hence, technologists use the word epoch to refer to checkpoints or time stamps that help organize and track the progress of technological development. Think of them as little milestones during training. It is like learning a new skill where you practice and get better in small steps, and after each step, you check how well you are doing. The first use of stone tools, around 3 million years ago, marks the beginning of the history of technology. Sharp stone flakes were used as knives, and larger, unsharpened stones were used as hammers to hunt. The oldest manufacturing invention is the Acheulean handaxe, the first tool built to butcher animals. By colliding two stones together, the early humans accidentally discovered fire. The Copper Age was an era of significant technological advantages. Humans extracted materials like copper and bronze to make tools. This hunter-gatherer phase of our history forms the first epoch of technology usage. During this epoch, the primary role of technology was to make human lives safer.

Acheulean hand tools dated 600,000–150,000 BCE

Nine Bifaces on view at The Met Fifth Avenue in Gallery 370

In the second epoch, several vital technologies came into being gradually with time. Instead of foraging, humans learned to settle down and grow crops through agriculture. They used clay for pottery and bricks. Not only this, clothing also began to be churned out of woven fabrics. People had to toil hard to provide for today's meal and the future. The Mesopotamian age witnessed significant technological advancements such as the first mass construction, water transportation, and irrigation. The Romans built roads, grand buildings, dams, reservoirs, and other sources of irrigation. The Classical Renaissance, a period spanning the 14th & 15th centuries, brought about many inventions, such as the printing press and telescope. The invention of the steam engine drove the progress in the early 18th century. The early part of the 20th century ushered in the era of fossil fuel-based transportation. This entire period, spanning 2500 BC till the middle of the 20th century, is the second epoch of technology usage, where humanity learned to harness naturally available energy sources mainly to reduce physical efforts.

The third epoch of technology usage spans from the middle of the 20th century till now. This epoch set the pace for the rapid digitalization of human lives. Through the adoption of computers, smartphones, internet & machine learning algorithms, we have benefitted in reducing our mental load. In stark contrast to the livelihood of our ancestors, we live in a time of extraordinarily fast technological change that has made our lives comfortable and well-connected.

It should be noted that the third epoch is unlike the earlier two epochs in many ways. Firstly, it is much shorter as compared to the earlier two epochs. During the first two epochs, humans used technology mainly to reduce physical efforts— stone or bronze hunting tools made hunting easier and more effective for our ancestors. Harnessing the power of water, steam, and fossil fuel-based electricity reduced our physical load manifold. It is interesting to note that in the first two epochs, the advantages of technology outweigh the disadvantages. Reducing physical burden allowed humans to spend more time and energy on thinking, creating, and contributing a lot to creating cultural artifacts. One can argue that physical load-reducing technologies in the first two epochs made humans less physically active and less fit, but lifestyle diseases emerged only in the 20th century.

In the third epoch, technology has been mainly used to reduce mental efforts. Calculators built into our smartphones have eliminated our need to calculate manually. It is easy to communicate with anyone worldwide without learning a new language just by using translation Apps. Computational problem-solving has become a breeze with the advent of computers. More recently, internet-based technologies have made it easy to search, share, and collaborate with anyone at any time.

Interestingly, the human body has had ample time to adjust in the first two epochs. Our brains, however, have yet to have enough time to change in the third epoch. The last twenty-odd years of the third epoch have also increased our cognitive load while at the same time reducing it elsewhere. For example, social media makes sharing opinions with many people easy. It would have been difficult or almost impossible to do so earlier unless you shouted at the top of your voice from a rooftop. However, social media also brings you hundreds of messages daily, and we are compelled to spend precious time reading and responding to them.

So, what happens next? I firmly believe in the current onset of the fourth epoch of technology usage. With advances in AI, and especially in Generative AI, technology has the potential to be our 24/7 co-pilot. We are looking at a future where the functioning of AI agents and humans will be intricately intertwined.

We are now part of a nonlinear world that increases the cognitive load on our brains. This "always-on, always-on-demand" characteristic has made us hyper-attentive and hyper-reactive. There is not enough time to do anything. We are always running behind the clock. The world is becoming difficult to navigate and is becoming increasingly nonlinear. Technology has undoubtedly helped us reap the benefits of modern civilization, where we all stand today. It has reshaped human history from the invention of wheels to the Industrial Revolution and has effectively made humanity reach many milestones. Technology will continue to change the world, and we must ensure it changes it for the better.

Technology Across Epochs

	Epoch 1	Epoch 2	Epoch 3	Epoch 4
Time period	Hunter-gatherer days of our ancestors before agriculture and permanent settlements came into being (from 2.5 Mn years BC till 2500 BC)	From 2500 BC till middle of 20th century	From middle of 20th century till now	
Primary role of technology	To make lives safe	Harnessing natural resources – readily available or processed – mainly to save physical efforts	Faster computation, data storage and transfer to drive digitalization and mass customization	
Examples of key technologies	Stone / bronze / iron tools for better hunting and protection	Domesticated animals for farming, water / steam power, electricity, internal combustion engines using fossil fuel, nuclear power	Computers, smartphones, internet, machine learning algorithms, social media	?
Impact on people	Less physical efforts to hunt, more physical safety	Less physical efforts, better quality of living, better physical connectivity	Better productivity, reducing mental load. At the same time increasing mental load	

Please join me as I take you through a journey starting with the impact of technology in today's increasingly nonlinear world. We will look at the potential of AI in leading us to a Digital Renaissance, and finally, we will look at the DeSIRe framework as a helpful guide on this exciting journey.

Happy Reading!

1

THE NONLINEAR WORLD

"The universe is so much bigger than you realize."

Alpha Waymond, *Everything Everywhere All at Once*

As you may know, the Oscar-winning movie *Everything Everywhere All at Once* is based on the idea of the 'multiverse', which entails the coexistence of unique multiple universes simultaneously and that each unique universe comprises 'reality' in that world. The multiverse concept has been explored across several comics, TV shows, and movies. The animated series *Rick and Morty* had its main characters communicate with different versions of themselves across the multiverse. Marvel Cinematic Universe has recently unlocked the gateway to box office success by popularizing the multiverse. Interestingly, the ideas about alternate realities are ancient and varied. In 1848, the author

Edgar Allan Poe wrote a prose poem in which he fancied the existence of "A limitless succession of Universes."

This book is not scholarly, scientific, or even a pop culture discourse on the multiverse. However, the multiverse concept offers a few pointers to our current world. We live in parallel coexisting realities in today's complex and physical world. There are moments we spend time in the physical world attending office or college in person, and there are other moments when we go virtual or digital while working or attending classes remotely. We are used to digital identities or avatars, and at the same time, we are equally comfortable in our own 100% natural skin. We use good old paper money and deal in digital money or cryptocurrency. Afterlife Apps allow us to live after we are dead. We make friends and unfriend people in the physical and digital worlds.

The third epoch of technology adoption led to this multiverse-like complexity. Technology is embedded in everything we use and function with daily. In all honesty, we cannot survive in this day and age without physical or digital technology. Let's examine the Internet of Things (IoT), which seamlessly links physical and digital technology. IoT refers to physical objects with sensors, processing ability, software, and other technologies that connect and exchange data with similar connective devices and systems over the Internet or other networks with connections. The idea of the Internet of Things first appeared in a speech by Peter T. Lewis. According to Lewis, *"The Internet of Things, or IoT, is the integration of people, processes, and technology with connectable devices and sensors to enable remote monitoring, status, manipulation and evaluation of trends of such devices."*

In 2004, Cornelius Peterson, then CEO of NetSilicon, predicted, "*The next era of information technology will be dominated by (IoT) devices, and networked devices will ultimately gain in popularity and significance to the extent that they will far exceed the number of networked computers and workstations.*" IoT devices are created for consumer use, including connected vehicles, wearable technology, connected health, and appliances with remote monitoring capabilities. These devices are now a part of the larger concept of home automation, which includes lighting, heating, air conditioning, security systems, and camera systems. Technology is already embedded in the human body through pacemakers and prosthetics. And we are just getting started. Nanotechnology will soon enhance human bodies & minds.

However, as much as technology has made our lives easier, it has also entangled us in various aspects.

Take a moment and look around— do you ever feel overwhelmed by the complexity of your world?

With modern technology advancing at an unprecedented pace, keeping up is becoming increasingly challenging. These are exciting times not just for technological development but also for technology policy—our technologies may be more advanced and complicated. Still, they need to be protected and sometimes even constrained. Just as our understanding of technology governance is developing in new and exciting ways, our understanding of emerging technologies' social, cultural, environmental, and political dimensions is also increasing. We are realizing both the challenges and the importance of mapping out the full range of ways technology is changing our society, what we want those changes to look like, and what tools we have to try to influence and guide those shifts.

Technologies are becoming increasingly complicated and interconnected at the same time. Cars, airplanes, medical devices, financial transactions, and electricity systems rely on more computer software than ever, making them seem more complicated to understand and control. Government and corporate surveillance of individuals and information processing relies largely on digital technologies and artificial intelligence and, therefore, involves less human-to-human contact and more opportunities for biases to be embedded and codified in our technological systems. Additionally, managing these systems is increasingly done through the cloud so that control over them is remote and removed from a direct human or social power. Now, we are ushering in the fourth epoch of technology adoption, so our world is transforming at an unprecedented pace. Technologies like artificial intelligence (AI), quantum computing, and nanotechnology are driving this transformation and are likely to fundamentally alter the way we live, work, function, and relate to one another.

But the technology that will have the most far-reaching impact on humanity will be AI - in general, and Generative AI - specifically. Several definitions of artificial intelligence (AI) have surfaced over the last few decades. John McCarthy (one of the founders of the discipline of Artificial Intelligence) offers the following definition— "It is the science and engineering of making intelligent machines, especially intelligent computer programs." The onset of artificial intelligence conversations was driven by Alan Turing's seminal work, "Computing Machinery and Intelligence," which was published in 1950. In this paper, Alan Turing asks the following question, "Can machines think?" From there, he offered a test, now famously known as the "Turing Test," where a human interrogator would try to distinguish between a computer and human response. While this test has been scrutinized since its publication, it remains a vital part of the history of Artificial Intelligence and current ethical discussions around Generative AI.

As we usher in the fourth epoch of technology adoption, all these new digital technologies are making our world increasingly nonlinear. But before we get into what is nonlinear, we must understand what is linear.

Linearity brings back childhood memories of our geometry classes in school. Linear refers to a straight line- the first thought that comes to our mind instantaneously. You must pass through point B to go from A to C as per geometric linearity. Any other variation is not possible in this linear world. However, this is geometry. Before the Internet surfaced and made our lives easier, we lived in an essentially linear and physical world.

Linearity 101

Arranged in a straight line, sequential, progressing from one stage to another in a series of steps, involving a single dimension

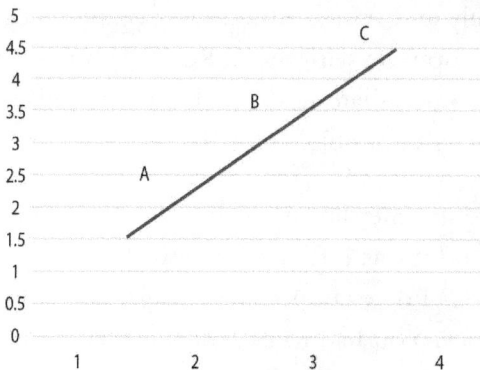

This pre-internet linear world has three characteristics:

- **First**, it was not easy to democratize or mass disseminate information. Information could only be shared instantaneously with a small number of people. One would have to wait for an advertisement, radio, or a news item to appear in print or TV to become aware of it. Notifications existed as bits and pieces picked up as gossip! One had to make efforts to meet people or to make friends.

- **Second**, customization for individual people at specific times was complicated. For example, everyone had access to the same or similar information. Hundreds of people reading a particular newspaper got the same information. Hundreds of people walking into a specific shop once saw the same brands, goods, and products. Hundreds of people entering a theater watched the same movie at that time.

- **Third**, there was no mass instant feedback loop. It was challenging to ask many people beyond your immediate family and friends about their opinions or even to share your opinion with them. Reaching a few strangers within your immediate circle of family, friends, and colleagues only was possible.

In the pre-internet linear world, everything took its own time and space, and it was difficult figuratively to skip B for you to go from A to C. For example, acquiring knowledge meant more formal studies. You had to experience everything firsthand, and it took time. However, today's nonlinear world is different. It seems effortless to democratize information. Anyone with a basic smartphone or laptop can reach millions of people instantaneously. Any individual with a basic smartphone has petabytes of information at their fingertips. We are just one click away from receiving or sending information— be it about booking a hotel, flight tickets, or planning a vacation, it is very simple. We can easily use WhatsApp, Messenger, and other communication platforms to contact anyone at any point in time and share the necessary information. Today, anything essential or unimportant can easily go viral within seconds and reach millions of people. Everyone is a receiver and could easily be a creator.

Customizing messages and delivery using powerful machine learning/AI algorithms is also very easy. Mass customization is the name of the game. Powerful algorithms used by technology companies such as Google, Amazon, YouTube, Spotify, and Netflix show customized content unique to you based on their understanding of your digital footprint.

Finally, there is an omnipresent instant feedback loop. Everything you do, express, and say in the nonlinear world leaves a digital footprint that could be used to influence your future attitudes, desires, and actions. If you post something on social media— photos, videos, or reels, you will get likes, comments, and even reposts immediately from strangers, acquaintances, and people you follow. If you want to sell your paintings, you can quickly post them on Facebook or Instagram and watch them go viral. If you want to promote your business, you can easily share your products online and reach thousands of people using the right strategies.

The genesis of our nonlinear world could be attributed to the third epoch of technology adoption. We largely had to deal with a linear and physical world during the first two epochs. With the third and upcoming fourth epoch, we not only have to live in two parallel physical and digital worlds but also deal with the different natures of the two worlds.

Our physical world largely stays linear, where you make real friends over time, have coffee with them in a coffee shop, and go to a physical shop to browse and buy things. In contrast, our digital world is increasingly nonlinear with hanging out with virtual friends in digital space and online browsing/shopping on various websites. In the linear world, there is an emphasis on processes and standardization (like having a standard layout in physical retail). In the nonlinear world, more emphasis is placed on customizable experience (unique layout in a digital shopping website or app customized to reflect your past choices and likes). In the linear world, there is less accumulation of data about our behavior. In the nonlinear world, we leave a much bigger digital footprint. The linear world is like slow-brewed coffee. The nonlinear world is instant coffee!

What is interesting is that all of us live these dual identities in these two worlds simultaneously. The linear world requires us to deploy more considered System 2 thinking. The nonlinear world is pacy and usually forces us into an intuitive and rapid System 1 thinking. The linear world usually has 'assembly line thinking,' which means it emphasizes specialization & "right first time." In contrast, the nonlinear world has "connecting the dots thinking" - it emphasizes generalizing & learning from mistakes and experiences. In contrast to the structured style of the linear world, the nonlinear world thrives on creativity.

Linear world	Nonlinear world
More physical world (physical retail, physical friends)	More digital world (eCommerce, connections)
Emphasis on processes (standard layout in physical retail)	Emphasis on experience (customized layout in digital retail)
More time / less data footprint (System 2)	Less time / more data footprint (System 1)
Assembly line thinking (emphasis on specialization & right first time)	Connecting the dots thinking (emphasis on generalizing & learning from mistakes and experiences)
Structured thinking (encourage compliance)	Creative thinking (encourage divergent thinking)
Consistency (same delivery to all people)	Customization (catered to individual needs)
One way / no feedback (TV viewing)	Two way / instant feedback (OTT / delayed viewing)

Moreover, linearity maintains consistency, meaning it ensures the same delivery to everyone. However, with nonlinearity, there is always an option for customization where you get to decide what you want. Lastly, there is no room for feedback in the linear world as it is a one-way process. For example, if you are watching TV, you can only record/download the shows you want to if you use a digital recorder or a set-top box. However, the nonlinear world is a two-way process. You can watch, download, and skip all your favorite shows whenever you want to on Netflix, Amazon Prime Video, and countless other platforms.

It is as if we live in a multiverse- two different worlds requiring two different ways of living. The concept of multiverse, as popularized by Marvel Cinematic Universe, *Rick & Morty,* or Oscar-winning movies such as *Everything Everywhere All At Once,* eliminates the need for linearity. If you want to go from A to C, you can hop into another universe and be at C without even visiting B. To be fair, multiverses exist only in our imagination for now, but in reality, nonlinearity has been increasing at a fast pace since early 2000.

Let us take a look at nonlinearity in today's world. It is rooted in technologies developed and launched in the last thirty years, which is a tiny fraction of humanity's existence on planet Earth over many millennia. Our minds have been subjected to this nonlinearity, complexity, and duality in a very short duration of humanity's timeline on earth. This wasn't the case with technologies of the first two epochs. An iron ax replaced a stone ax. Cars using internal combustion engines replaced horse-drawn carriages. Only in the last few decades have we experienced linear and nonlinear worlds coexist, and we have to straddle both of them. We have experienced linearity for a much greater length of time as compared to the recent blip of nonlinearity. The level and impact of nonlinearity will increase manifolds as we enter the fourth epoch. This increasing nonlinearity has a profound and lasting impact on our minds and how we think. In the next chapter, we will dive into this impact in detail.

2

IMPACT OF TECHNOLOGY ON OUR MINDS

In today's era, digital technologies are used to track and diagnose agriculture, health, and environmental issues. They can be used to defend human rights, including data privacy— but they can also be used to violate them, for example, by monitoring our movements, purchases, conversations, and behaviors without consent. Governments and businesses increasingly have the tools to mine and exploit data for financial and other purposes. From video and computer games to smart televisions, a wide range of technological inventions have helped us engage our free time and grow apart from people at the same time. Watching movies is no longer limited to a theater space. The way we read on a computer, we watch movies on digital platforms and read books on Kindle. Online streaming platforms and applications are moving the entertainment world to a complete digitization mode.

Although several people argue against technology, there is no doubt that we, as human beings, cannot function the way we do today without technology. We could not enjoy the same standard of living & luxury, and we could not enjoy our leisure time nearly as much. For example, with the advent of modern cars, we can journey in a fraction of the time it takes to walk or even ride a bike. This undeniably indicates that our lives have been made much easier by the utility of cars. After that, smartphones and the internet allow us to garner a wealth of knowledge at our fingertips, the ability to almost flawlessly contact friends and family from afar, and to save time and money by doing things from our home as opposed to doing things by having to leave, waste fuel driving, reach our destination, wait in line for a half an hour, and hopefully get what we are looking for.

It is no secret that technology is changing the way we behave. But it is also changing the way we think and process information. We are constantly plugged in and connected to the digital world, from social media to smartphones. If we take a look at the episode of Nosedive from the Netflix show *Black Mirror,* written by Charlie Brooker, it reflects the world we live in and how social media impacts our lives. It shows how much a person can go just to attain social validation. This dystopian series has portrayed the not-so-near future. From virtual reality that gets a bit too real to the horror of artificial intelligence and spending life after death living in a simulation, Black Mirror is often eerily realistic. It compels us to consider how technology can affect society and transform our behavior and minds. But before we delve further into the impact of technology on our minds, it is essential to understand what makes us humans.

Robert Oppenheimer, the inventor of the atomic bombs, said, *"I have become death, the destroyer of worlds."* The two nuclear bombs dropped on Hiroshima and Nagasaki in 1945 killed around 200,000 people. No other species has ever wielded such power, and no species could. The technology behind the atomic bomb exists due to a cooperative hive mind— hundreds of scientists and engineers worked together to form it. The same unique intelligence and cooperation also underly more positive advances, such as modern medicine. To cut it short, humans are both the destroyer and preserver, with technology as the enabler.

Physiologically, we have characteristics that are more or less unique to our species- opposable thumbs and how our larynx is built to allow us to talk and stand upright. There are numerous theories about what makes us human. The topic of human existence has been pondered for millions of years. Ancient Greek philosophers like Socrates, Plato, and Aristotle had theorized about the nature of human existence, as have countless philosophers since then. Aristotle said that we are rational animals and pursue knowledge for its own sake. While there may be no concrete conclusion, there is no doubt that humans are unique creatures. What makes us human is language, self-awareness, and the ability to imagine. We live by art and reasoning.

One key characteristic that makes us human is that we can think about alternative futures and make deliberate choices accordingly. Creatures without such a capacity cannot be bound into a social contract or take moral responsibility. Once we become aware of what we cause, we may feel morally obliged to change our ways. We are the only species on this planet with the foresight capable of deliberately plotting a path toward a desirable long-term future. Ian Tattersall says, *"Obviously, we have*

98.8% close and yet to so different!

Photo by Francesco Ungaro on Unsplash

similarities. We have similarities with everything else in nature; it would be astonishing if we didn't. But we've got to look at the differences."

Comparative studies between humans and chimps indicate that while both will cooperate, humans will always tend to help more. Children seem to be innate helpers. They act selflessly before social norms set in. They have more compassion and empathy than adults. Not only this, studies have shown that they will spontaneously open doors for adults and pick up "accidentally" dropped items. They will even stop playing to help. They can quickly put a smile on anybody's face. Their sense of fairness begins young. Even if an experiment is unfairly rigged so that one child receives more rewards, they will ensure a reward is fairly split. John Straughton says, *"There are a number of things that make us human and separate us from animals. One is our ability to self-analyze and engage in mental time travel. We can also imagine different scenarios and reason abstractly. Additionally, we have established cultures with rules and moral codes. Finally, our brain functions allow us to learn rapidly and make decisions based on more than just survival instincts."*

Our mental abilities have allowed us to tame fire and invent the wheel. We survive by our wits. Our minds have shaped civilizations and technologies that have changed the face of the Earth. As humans, we learn from our past experiences. We are always open to new information. We process this further information while considering past learnings and can imagine possibilities for the future and make informed decisions about the future. We can also communicate these thoughts with other humans. To all of this, we use System 1 vs. System 2 thinking. The concept of two thinking systems, System 1 and System 2 thinking, was put forth by the Nobel Prize winner and the intellectual godfather of behavioral economics, Daniel Kahneman, in the book *Thinking, Fast & Slow*. He and his great collaborator Amos Tversky framed human thinking in two forms that they call *System 1* and *System 2.*

According to Kahneman and Tversky, human judgment and decision-making, with all of its biases and heuristics, could be explained within the two-system view:

a) **System 1 thinking is a near-instantaneous process**; it happens automatically, intuitively, and with little effort. It is driven by instinct and our experiences. It is frugal to use mental energy.

b) **System 2 thinking is slower and requires more effort and mental energy**. It is conscious and logical and requires significant cognitive effort and puts a strain on our minds.

While traveling for work, you know which route to take without having to think about it consciously. You automatically walk to the subway station, get off at the same stop, and walk to your office while your mind wanders. It is absolutely effortless. However, the subway line is down today. While your route to the subway station was intuitive, you now find yourself analyzing alternative routes to work to take the quickest one. Are the buses running? Is it too cold or hot outside to walk? How much does a rideshare cost?

Before the advent of today's technology, the application of both systems was more streamlined for most of the last two millennia. For system 1— We see a snake, and our experience/learning tells us to avoid it. Or, say we want to make a low-value purchase (a candy) and instinctively pick up a sweet in a red wrapper. For System 2 — If we're going to learn a new language-Well, we learned this in school, took a language class, read books in the new language, and spoke to people who already know the language. Thus, System 1 thrives on nonlinearity, while System 2 thrives on linearity. In an increasingly nonlinear world, it is different.

Nonlinearity can unnecessarily trigger system 1— every social media post requires views. Every comment requires a response. Sharing something is more critical than enjoying it, etc. Moreover, many decisions may be taken out of impulse based on an artificial sense of urgency. Again, System 1 thinking operates automatically and quickly, with little effort and no sense of voluntary control. For example, it can be done quickly if you are asked to detect an object farther than another, see sadness in somebody's voice, or drive a car on an empty road. However, System 2 thinking allocates attention to activities that demand effort, including complex computations. It is often associated with the subjective experience of agency, choice, and concentration. For example, if you focus your attention on a particular individual in a crowd, walk faster than average, monitor your behavior in a social situation, or multiply 1776 x 2489, these things require some mental activities and proper effort.

While it is true that the unique human ability to reason allows for science, technology, and advanced problem-solving, there are limitations to reason in today's nonlinear world. Today's technology spoon-feeds our minds too much at times, thus eliminating or reducing the need to think. Googling takes precedence over trying to recall. Using a calculator takes over even the simple act of adding 34 to 89. Highly deliberative people often tend to be less empathetic, are often perceived as less trustworthy, and this can undermine their influence.

One needs to manage one's digital persona to stay in the race. 'Instagrammability' of a beautiful sunset or a mouthwatering plate of food takes precedence over enjoying these. Indeed, the ability of human beings to be rational has seemingly had a tough run. Misinformation is spreading quickly on social media, political polarization is rising, and science is being ignored. The much-lauded ability for humans to stop and reflect is not winning in the battle against the very human tendency to rely on our gut feelings and intuitions in the nonlinear world. We should be more mindful of what we expect from our cognition. The question is not whether we should trust our ability to reason or our intuition; instead, we can find agreement between what our heart wants and what our reason says. Galileo once noted that "where the senses fail us, reason must step in," a conclusion consistent with that of Kahneman's *Thinking, Fast and Slow*. Galileo and Kahneman are correct; of course, it is not the answer to the entire puzzle. Perhaps we must add, "Where reason fails us, our intuitions must step in."

The negative impact of technology in the nonlinear world can be categorized into two areas:

1) **Reduction in our attention spans**: Too many stimuli are fighting for our attention. Individual customization of the stimulus increases the craving to do more and reduces attention to the present task at hand even more. The impact of interruptions on individual productivity can also be catastrophic. On average, we experience an interruption every eight minutes or about seven or eight interruptions per hour. In an eight-hour day, that is about 60 interruptions. With the extensive usage of social media, most youngsters find it hard to concentrate. Many students will study for barely fifteen minutes and hop on their phones to check if their posts have received likes, shares, or comments.

In an article, Nicholas Carr says (before publishing his book *The Shallow*), "*Immersing myself in a book or a lengthy article used to be easy. My mind would get caught up in the narrative or the turns of the argument, and I'd spend hours strolling through long stretches of prose. That's rarely the case anymore. Now my concentration often starts to drift after two or three pages. I get fidgety, lose the thread, and begin looking for something else to do. I feel as if I'm always dragging my wayward brain back to the text. The deep reading that used to come naturally has become a struggle.*" Repeated interruptions often affect concentration. Persistent interruptions and distractions at work are bound to have a profound effect. It can affect a person's lifestyle and even their sleep pattern.

Excessive and pathological usage of the internet or technology can lead to frequent mood changes, development of intolerance, withdrawal, and functional impairment. Screen time may also adversely impact cognitive and brain development. In today's generation, even toddlers are addicted to smartphones. Young parents find it easy to hand over a video game, smartphone, or tablet to quieten the child from creating a stir. While it helps temporarily, it will likely affect the child as they grow up. In children of preschool age and older, digital media directed towards active learning can be fruitful and educational, but only when it is accompanied by parental interaction with the teacher. The global prevalence of internet addiction is estimated at 6%, but in some regions, such as the Middle East, the majority is as high as 11%. Students with internet addiction have a higher chance of suffering from ADHD symptoms such as inattention, hyperactivity, and impulsivity. People with ADHD symptoms have a greater risk of developing technology addiction.

To dig deeper into the impact of today's technology on human attention, let us take a look at the four types of attention we use during our daily activities— **Sustained attention, Selective attention, Alternating attention, and Divided attention.**

a) **Sustained attention** is the ability to focus on a particular task for long hours without getting distracted. It also refers to maintaining vigilance or alertness. However, a recent study demonstrated that sustained attention ability is predicted by whole-brain functional connectivity during rest and that only 27% of high sustained attention network edges were located within frontoparietal regions. Sustained attention indicates the ability to sustain attention over time in specific goal-directed behaviors. For example, students at school need to have sustained attention when they are in class if they want to excel in academics because poor sustained attention could result in below-average performance. Most of the tasks that we come across in our daily lives require a certain level of sustained attention, whether it be watching a movie, making food, completing an assignment, or meeting deadlines. In fact, since you are already in the second chapter of this book, you are using your sustained attention.

b) **Selective attention:** is the ability to select from many factors and focus only on one thing at a time while filtering other distractions. At any given point in time, we are subjected to a constant barrage of sensory overload- The blare of a motorcycle from the street, the chatter of your friends, fights between neighbors, the sound of the whistle, the clicks of the typewriter, the hum of a fan or air-conditioner. In certain cases, we do not pay any heed to each and every one of these sensory experiences. Instead, we focus our attention on the important elements of our environment while other things blend into the background. So, the real question is— how do we decide what to pay attention to and what to avoid? Well, this is an example of selective attention because our ability to attend to the things around us is limited in terms of both capacity and duration. Thus, we must be picky about what we pay attention to. In his text Cognition: Theory and Practice, author Russell Revlin explains, *"To sustain our* *attention to one event in everyday life, we must filter out other events. We must be selective in our attention by focusing on some events to the detriment of others. This is because attention is a resource that needs to be distributed to those events that are important."*

c) **Alternating attention**: It is the ability to switch our focus back and forth between tasks that require our cognitive demands. Therefore, mental flexibility is required to enable the switch and to perform multiple tasks efficiently without the cognitive load of one task limiting the performance of the others. Well, we use alternating attention more often than we realize. For example, you switch your focus between taking notes from the lecture in class and making sense of those notes during the class or a presentation. Again, if you are heating vegetable soup on the stove, that requires stirring from time to time; when you are not stirring the soup, you are chopping other ingredients, which will later be added to the soup. Thus, here, two tasks require attention— stirring and chopping, and each requires carrying out a pattern of movements and a different cognitive load. Although this may seem like two relatively simple tasks, this would be very complicated for people with difficulties in alternating attention because they need more time to shift their focus and pick up and initiate new task requirements.

d) **Divided attention** is simultaneously processing two or more responses. It is often referred to as multitasking. Divided attention is a type of simultaneous attention that allows us to process different information sources and successfully carry out multiple tasks simultaneously. This critical cognitive skill allows us to be more efficient in our daily lives. You use divided attention when you focus on two or more elements simultaneously. You are essentially dividing your attention between two or more tasks. Well, divided attention requires focus on a large scale by not permitting us to focus fully on any task. For example, you may have written an email while attending a meeting, finished an assignment while listening to music, completed your homework while watching a football match, eaten your dinner while watching a show on Netflix, etc. Again, a waiter must use their divided attention when attending to a table. They have to remember what the man at table 5 wanted, write down the order for table 7, and be careful to balance the plates of food that they are holding. While divided attention may be affected by psychiatric conditions like schizophrenia or Attention Deficit Hyperactive Disorder (ADHD), it mostly affects general attention. It is also quite common to have attentional problems after suffering from a Traumatic Brain Injury (TBI) or stroke. However, in these cases, the attentional alteration and its sub-components may vary, depending on the affected brain areas.

While sustained and selective attention are less impacted by today's technology, alternating and divided attention are more impacted by today's technology. In her book *'Attention Span,'* Gloria Mark mentions her research— *"Our attention spans have declined over two decades, averaging just 47 seconds on any screen."*

Reduced attention spans could result in non-informed or ill-informed opinions, which can be easily shared over social media. Reduced attention spans could hinder deeper understanding. Gloria Mark further says, *"We are experiencing a fundamental shift in how we think, how we work, how we focus, and how we achieve fulfillment. We can all feel it—in our burnout, Zoom fatigue, endless notifications, and our inability to maintain our attention. Technology has been designed with the intent to augment our capabilities and help us produce more, but we are also distracted and exhausted in our everyday use with it. It might feel like we are losing our ability to focus entirely, but there is some good news. Our ability to focus isn't lost, the way we focus is just changing."*

In her book, Gloria Mark debunks the myth that we must always strive to be focused and should feel guilty if we cannot concentrate. However, just as we cannot lift weights for long periods, we cannot hold sustained focus for long stretches. In both cases, we will need rest to replenish our resources. She also refutes the myth that mindless activities on our phones are a waste of time. Sometimes, mindless activities like playing simple games do not just make us temporarily happy. When used strategically, those activities can help us replenish our overspent mental resources and enable fresh ideas to surface. The third myth the author discredits is that our distractions and inability to focus on our devices are primarily due to our lack of discipline. However, it is more complicated than that. Several underlying socio-technical forces lead us to be distracted. The last myth that the author debunks is the much-popularized idea that "Flow is the ideal state we should strive for when we use our technologies." Well, rather than trying to achieve flow, which is not realistic for the nature of most of our jobs, which require an analytical mindset, our goal instead should be to achieve a balance of different types of attentional states. In our always-on, always-connected nonlinear world, alternating and divided attention is an easy casualty. We default to shallow and trigger-happy decision-making to cope with the demands of the nonlinear world.

2) **Shallow and trigger-happy decision making—** Information overload & reduced attention spans lead to a false criticality & immediacy of deciding. Reduced attention is universal and will lead to more severe problems for sustained technology exposure & abuse like impaired emotional and social intelligence, technology addiction, social isolation, adverse impact on brain and cognitive development, and lack of proper sleep. Young, developing brains are susceptible to chronic exposure to computers, smartphones, tablets, or televisions. Children who practically survive on smartphones all day will likely have impaired memories or patience in the long run. They might even fail to concentrate and make the right choices in life due to this overdose of technology. Some people find it difficult to initiate a conversation with any individual due to a lack of social intelligence and might feel ostracized. Ninety percent of young adults use social media platforms such as Facebook, Twitter, Snapchat, TikTok, and Instagram on a regular basis. Paradoxically, social media usage is linked to social isolation as you barely experience human communication. Not only this, the overuse of technology can affect a human being's sleep pattern and disturb the rest they require. But the biggest impact is on our ability to use deliberate system 2 thinking as we default to shallow and trigger-happy decision-making.

Now, if we ask ourselves— what is the outcome of reduced attention span & shallow trigger-happy decision-making?

Well, the outcome has resulted in the rewiring of our brains-the way we think, the way we decide, etc. Just as our muscles can be built or get atrophied by over-stimulation or under-stimulation, our brains will undergo changes with reduced attention or shallow trigger-happy decision-making. Our bodies have evolved over time due to the impact of earlier technologies. The latest technologies are just thirty years old. So, the changes will be more Cambrian in nature. These changes in attention can affect our brains, which brings us to the topic of Neuroplasticity-It is the brain's ability to change and adapt due to experience.

The term "Plasticity" was first applied to behavior in 1890 by William James in *The Principles of Psychology,* where the term was used to describe *"A structure weak enough to yield to an influence, but strong enough not to yield all at once."* It is an umbrella term referring to the brain's ability to change, reorganize, or grow neural networks. This can involve functional changes due to brain damage or structural changes due to learning. The first few years of a child's life are a time of rapid brain growth. At birth, every neuron in the cerebral cortex has an estimated 2,500 synapses or small connections between neurons where nerve impulses are relayed. By age three, this number has grown to a whopping 15,000 synapses per neuron. Neuroplasticity is most active in childhood as a part of normal human development and can also be seen as an important mechanism for children in terms of risk and resiliency. As our brains get re-wired to cope with the nonlinearity, there is a risk that the balance between system 1 & system 2 thinking may become unstable, especially as the nonlinearity increases daily. What makes us human- our ability to reason or imagine- may come under pressure as the nonlinearity around us grows.

However, it is not an entirely doomsday scenario for us. There are certain benefits like achieving more out of life — A lot of people can perform multiple tasks at their jobs, often at the same time, a process called multitasking. Multitasking is a valuable skill in many industries, as it increases productivity and saves time. The art of learning how to develop this ability can help one acquire better concentration skills. Multitasking refers to the ability to manage multiple responsibilities at once by focusing on one task while keeping track of others. In the workplace, multitasking often involves switching back and forth between tasks based on their importance and urgency. For example, answering the phone in a busy reception area while writing emails shows multitasking skills.

Then, we could reduce our cognitive loads with the adoption of Generative AI to take on repetitive mundane tasks. Apart from multitasking & reducing cognitive load, there is improvement in reaction time, better insight/self-awareness (sleep monitoring could lead to better sleep hygiene), the potential for better decision-making due to access to more information, and the unlocking of creativity if time is freed up. Hence, there is a silver lining. Today's technology *per se* is a good thing. Technology has also made our lives easier, faster, better, and more fun in many ways.

Just as System 1 and System 2 thinking can co-exist, focused-deep-long attention and peripheral-shallow-short attention can co-exist as long as we exercise control on when to use what. However, this is different from technologies from the first two epochs, where the primary objective of technology was to reduce physical load. The technology of the modern era (whether from the third epoch or the upcoming fourth epoch) can reduce and add to cognitive load. Our increasingly nonlinear world is putting tremendous pressure on our brains. Like any other technology, this comes with some advantages and disadvantages. The key will be to harness the positives and control the negatives. But it is easier said than done. We are at a tipping point. The fourth epoch of technology adoption is just around the corner. The latest advances in Generative Artificial Intelligence (Generative AI) will increase the impact of today's technology manifolds in the next few years. In the next chapter, we look at how Generative AI differs from other technologies from the third epoch and how it will propel us into the fourth epoch of technology adoption.

3

THE RISE OF ARTIFICIAL INTELLIGENCE (AI)

"Any sufficiently advanced technology is equivalent to magic."

- Arthur C. Clarke

Artificial Intelligence (AI) has become one of the most talked-about topics of today. AI is revolutionizing how we live and work, from self-driving cars to virtual assistants. AI has existed for some time, yet it is evolving fast. As mentioned in the previous chapters, the term Artificial Intelligence (AI) was first coined by John McCarthy in 1956, when he held the first academic conference on the subject. However, the journey to understand if machines can honestly think began before that. In Vannevar Bush's seminal work, *As We May Think,* he proposed a system that amplifies people's knowledge and understanding.

Alan Turing had written a paper on the notion of machines being able to simulate human beings and the ability to do intelligent things, such as play chess.

Well, it is vital to understand what the rise of artificial intelligence (AI) means for our future. Within a short span, AI has taken the world by storm, and it feels like magic. Several people need to become more familiar with the concept of artificial intelligence (AI). As an illustration, when 1,500 senior business leaders in the United States in 2017 were asked about AI, only 17 percent said they knew what it meant. Many of them needed clarification on what it was and how it would affect their particular companies. They understood there was considerable potential for altering business processes but it needed to be more apparent to them how Artificial Intelligence (AI) could be deployed within their organizations. Recent studies indicate that though the awareness of AI has increased substantially, people still need help thinking about current successful applications of AI and have difficulty imagining expected future ones, too. Stephen Hawking warned: *"Strong AI would take off on its own and redesign itself at an ever-increasing rate. Humans, who are limited by slow biological evolution, couldn't compete, and would be superseded."* We must be ready to make the most of what is coming up!

If computers can undoubtedly follow instructions and do computations faster than humans, can computers think & feel like humans? For this, computers need not have to depend on instructions provided by humans all the time. Nobody can refute the ability of a computer to process logic. However, thinking goes beyond just following logic or just pre-decided steps. The precise definition of 'think' becomes essential to answer the question of whether computers can think. For example, there is the 'Chinese room' argument— Let us imagine someone is locked in a room where they were passed notes in Chinese. Even if they use an entire library of rules and lookup tables, they could produce valid responses in Chinese. However, would they really 'understand' the language, cultural codes, and nuances and grasp all of these without stepping out of the room? The argument is that since computers would constantly be applying rote fact lookup, they could never 'understand' a subject the way only a human would do.

In 1950, rudimentary electronic computers were starting to emerge, and the concept of artificial intelligence was almost entirely theoretical. In the same year, the Turing test was proposed. The question was— will we ever build a computer that can imitate a human so well that we cannot tell the difference? Alan Turing could only explore his inquiry with a thought experiment— The Imitation Game. The game, commonly known as the Turing test, is simple. One person, player E, is an evaluator who poses written questions to players A and B in different rooms. Out of A and B, one is human, and the other is a computer. Now, the objective is for the evaluator to determine which player is the computer. He can only try to decipher a computer and a human by asking the players questions and evaluating the "humanness" of their written responses.

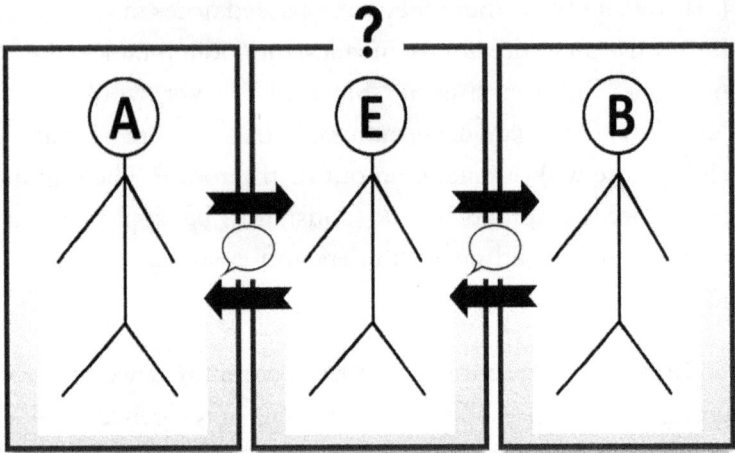

The Turing Test

If the computer can fool the interrogator into thinking its responses were generated by a human, it passes the Turing test. After all, it might be fundamentally impossible to know what is happening in the 'mind' of a computer, and even if computers do think, the process might be fundamentally different from that of the human brain. Hence, Alan Turing replaced his original question with one we have an answer to: *"Are there imaginable computers which would do well in the imitation game?"* This is one question that established a standard for assessing the sophistication of computers— a challenge that has inspired computer scientists and AI researchers over the past few decades.

Claude Shannon wrote a paper about developing a chess-playing program much before the days of high-speed computing arrived. As computing speeds increased & it was possible to store large amounts of data, computers got better at computation tasks such as playing chess. However, it is crucial to remember that these tasks were primarily computational. These programs could instantaneously evaluate millions of chess moves and decide on the best one, and by winning against humans, computers just exhibited their superior computing & storage advantage. But, even at that time, to the world, a computer beating a world chess champion was magical. Well, chess has always been considered a game of intellect, and many pioneers of computing felt that a chess-playing machine would be the hallmark of accurate artificial intelligence. While the Turing Test is a challenge to ascertain machine intelligence, being good at chess does not make computers intelligent in a general sense.

Now, the question is— what has changed in the past twenty years? In the past twenty years, three things have changed:

1) **Data explosion -** With the rise of smartphones and the internet, the data we generate daily is humongous. The term' Big Data' refers to the quantum of data and the diversity of data. Most of this data is unstructured- images, videos, and voice. Patrick Smith says, *"It is a world of unstructured data, not blocks or databases."* Social media user-generated data, search engine data, healthcare data, astronomical data, and real-time data such as the information provided by Global Positioning Systems- there is an explosion in data! The ultimate goal of working with big data is to extract useful information. With around 4.66 billion active Internet users worldwide, daily data surpasses one's imagination. For example, 404,444 users streamed on Netflix every minute. (Domo, 2020). People send 500 million tweets daily. (TechJury, 2020). Three hundred hours of video were uploaded on YouTube per minute (e-Learning Infographics, 2020). These numbers

keep on increasing all the time as more and more people have access to high quality internet and smartphones.

2) **Increase in computing power** - During an interview in 1970, the founder of Intel Corporation, Gordon E. Moore, was asked to estimate the growth of computing technology. He had stated that the number of transistors in an integrated circuit would double every two years. This bold prediction has been proven true for decades, and despite many claims that it is dead and obsolete, Intel CEO Brian Krzanich stated in January 2017 that "Moore's Law is alive and well and flourishing." Denizens of Silicon Valley have called Moore's Law "the most important graph in human history." Economists have found that Moore's Law powered the computing revolution and has been one of the most important sources of national productivity growth. Computing power connects our world's real (chip energy) and virtual (algorithm) dimensions. It is an intangible asset that can be used and circulated. It is a remarkable innovation for humankind and an upgrade for the digital economy. One can only do with massive computing power if one needs to handle vast data. Cloud computing has ensured enormous computing power is available to many users without considerable investment.

3) **The advent of machine learning algorithms** - With the advent of machine learning algorithms, especially the ones using unsupervised/reinforced learning, a lot of data is input into computers with massive computing power to let them learn without providing explicit instructions. Machine learning (ML) is an algorithm that automatically improves itself through a process of learning (whether

supervised or unsupervised) and does not require detailed instructions every time data is processed. The algorithm obtains experience by processing more and more data and then fine-tuning itself based on the properties of the outcome. There are three general machine learning techniques—

a. **Reinforcement learning**: The algorithm performs actions that will get rewarded the most. It is often used by game-playing AI or navigational robots.

b. **Unsupervised machine learning**: The algorithm finds patterns in unlabeled data by clustering and identifying similarities. A few popular uses include recommendation systems and targeted advertising.

c. **Supervised machine learning**: Here, the algorithm analyzes labeled data and learns how to map input data to an output label. It is used for classification and prediction.

With these three factors, we have taken our first steps in getting computers to think like humans. The human child takes in data through all her senses and learns independently. Sometimes, a human child needs reinforcement (positive or negative) or supervision to fast-track learning. Dr. John Kelly of IBM estimates that a whopping 90% of the world's data is dark, indicating that humans and computers cannot use it meaningfully. Meanwhile, the Internet of Things (IoT) will add more to that cache as numerous new devices go online regularly. *"The future of computing will not—and cannot—be based on ever-increasing processing power,"* says Shawn Kim, the Head of the Asia

Technology team. *"Instead, it will rely on understanding and drawing inferences from massive collections of data."*

Simply put, computers that can use data to learn, adapt, evolve, and 'think' will mimic the human brain. For a long time, we have been familiar with the power of machine learning algorithms- when we shop on eCommerce sites, use Google Maps for navigation, or use Google Search. This was the early stage of AI, but with one considerable caution. You could only talk to a computer through code and not the way you talk to another human being- using language. Natural Language Processing (NLP) and Computer Vision, the next developments, ensured that computers started processing human languages, images, and videos to go beyond structured data.

The advances in NLP and Computer Vision fast-tracked Generative AI. It became much easier to process language, image, and sound data. Generative AI- the newest kid on the block- has taken the world by storm from last year. ChatGPT (which quickly reached 100 mn user status) symbolizes the excitement around generative AI. Three critical factors have contributed to the excitement around using or deploying Generative AI:

1) **Low / no programming experience is required to use or deploy Generative AI -** Anyone with a computer or smartphone can use it as you engage with it, just like you speak to a human being. For the first time, the field of AI has been democratized. Recall the discussion around the internet being a great leveler at the beginning of the third epoch. Generative AI plays the same role at the beginning of the fourth epoch.

2) **Generative AI is human-like to interact with -** You interact with Generative AI in human language, and it recognizes your tonality and emotions. It could be asked to respond in a way you want to understand and in a comfortable tone, and it is a game-changer. For the first time, humans and computing systems will have a closer connection, and computing systems will feel human-like. This is the moment when computing systems using Generative AI could pass the Turing test easily.

3) **Easy availability of pre-trained models of Generative AI -** Generative AI uses pre-trained foundational models (called Large Language Models - LLMs in short) that could be used as the base to build specific applications. We don't need to start from scratch every time; we can use this foundation to build further on. These foundational models are based on 'transformers', deep learning models. Transformers were first introduced in 2017 and are becoming the model of choice for Generative AI as they efficiently use the self-attention mechanism, differentially weighting the significance of each part of the input data, text, or images.

Self-attention helps the LLM model understand the relationships between different words (tokens) in a sentence. Imagine you have a sentence: "The cat sat on the mat." Each word in this sentence is a token. Self-attention allows the LLM to give importance to each token based on its relevance to the others. The LLM uses three components to calculate self-attention: query, key, and value. Let us say the query is "Cat." The LLM compares the query with all other tokens (keys) in the sentence. It calculates the similarity between the query and each key. For example, the similarity between "cat" and "cat" is high because they are similar. However, the similarity between "cat" and "mat" might be lower because they are not closely related.

The cat sat on the mat

Most of us will visualize this

Some of us may get creative in visualizing

Created using DALL.E 2

Once the LLM calculates the similarity scores, a scaling operation is applied to ensure they are not too large. These scores are then used to weigh the importance of each token (value) in the sentence. The LLM combines the values using the attention scores to generate a more contextual representation of the sentence. In this way, self-attention helps LLMs capture dependencies between words and improve their understanding of language. These LLM-based foundation models are pre-trained using large data sets (100,000 books, for example). This way, the model 'knows' that 'the cat sat on the mat' makes sense, but 'Sat mat the cat on' has no meaning. This is precisely how human beings learn. We 'know' that 'mat' will be the missing word in the sentence 'the cat sat on the ...' Now, with Generative AI, this 'knowledge' is stored and readily available for anyone.

Here is another example of self-attention, but referring to Computer Vision (visual data). Imagine you are driving but waiting at a red light, and this is what you see in front of you. You 'know' that the red light is your first priority and that you should not move unless it turns green. You also know that you should watch out for the elderly couple as they may still be crossing the road when the light turns green (you have factored in your past knowledge that older people walk slowly and may take longer to cross the road). You intuitively know that the guy with the cap on the left has already crossed, and he is not likely to interfere with your driving when you start. Also, you certainly know that you should not waste your time looking at distant skyscrapers and flying airplanes as they have nothing to do with your driving and the road ahead of you.

How do we, humans, 'know this'? We have learned this over time, and each of us has a unique foundation model of the world in our heads. This is precisely what Generative AI is mimicking to do. Before transformers, algorithms would take all visual data

from the picture above and treat it equally after breaking it into individual pixels. This is not efficient and does not reflect how humans see or drive. We are sensitive to any movement. We have peripheral vision. All this allows us to autonomously divert more attention to things that matter while driving (a large building is less critical while driving than an elderly couple crossing the street, though the large building will take a much bigger share of our view).

The good part about generative AI is that it mimics human-like thinking. The not-so-good part is that human thinking comes with flaws or biases, and Generative AI will also learn these biases over time.

In the last five years, we have made great advances. Earlier algorithms were more suited for structured data. With transformer-based algorithms driving Generative AI, computers' ability to process unstructured data (pictures, videos, language, and music) has increased substantially. Now, computers can converse like humans (ChapGPT), create pictures based on language prompts (Dall e-2, Midjourney), and compose music. In a way, computers are becoming more human-like in the Generative AI world. Generative AI is the newest mass technology on the block- the fastest to reach a 100 mm user base, and it is taking the world by storm.

Any new technology immediately raises concerns, and given that most technologies have taken some work away from humans, the same situation is being talked about for generative AI. Will it replace humans?

Artificial Intelligence is making our world even more nonlinear, and we should be aware of it. It is possible that AI could replace humans in some industries, particularly for tasks that are repetitive, dangerous, time-consuming, or require a high degree of precision. For example, AI-powered robots are increasingly being used to perform tasks such as assembly, painting, and welding in manufacturing. In customer service, AI-powered chatbots can handle simple inquiries, but more complex issues still require human intervention. AI algorithms can help detect fraud in the financial industry, but human analysts are still needed to interpret the results and make decisions. In a way, Artificial Intelligence (AI) is likely to change the nature of work in many industries rather than replace human workers completely. As AI becomes more advanced, it is natural for humans to be freed up from performing repetitive tasks and will instead focus on higher-level, creative, and strategic work.

The latest advances in Generative AI will increase the impact of today's technology on us manifolds in the next few years. AI can potentially lead us to a Digital Renaissance, or it could lead to Digital Dystopia. The next chapter will look at the Digital Renaissance in the fourth epoch of technology adoption.

4

USHERING DIGITAL RENAISSANCE

"History doesn't repeat itself, but it often rhymes"

– Mark Twain.

When you book a hotel/homestay via an application, AI calculates the best dynamic fare for you and instructs you on how much to pay. When you book a table at a restaurant via a food delivery application, an AI guides you in completing your booking based on your past choices and likes. When you enter an airport, an AI-enabled security system scrutinizes what you do. To put it straight— we are increasingly being surrounded by AI everywhere. As discussed in the previous chapters, AI has become one of the most discussed topics in the digital age. From self-driving cars to virtual assistants to the latest advances in

Generative AI like ChatGPTs or Midjourney, AI is revolutionizing how we function in our daily lives. However, as much as AI has made our lives easier in ample ways, it is necessary to understand what the rise of AI indicates for our future. Edward Fredkin mentions that *"Artificial intelligence is the next stage in evolution,"* an idea first proposed by Samuel Butler's **Darwin Among the Machines** and expanded upon by George Dyson in 1998.

Though AI has been around for a while now, the latest advances in Generative AI have opened up the possibility of humankind entering a period of Digital Renaissance. But before we look at what this Digital Renaissance could look like, let's travel back in time to 14th-16th century Europe to get a flavor of Classical Renaissance, as the upcoming Digital Renaissance shares a lot of commonalities with what happened way back in the 15th century.

The Sistine Chapel ceiling painted in fresco by Michelangelo between 1508 and 1512

Photo by Calvin Craig on Unsplash

The Classical Renaissance was a cultural, socio-political movement that profoundly impacted the entire human civilization, although it began in Italy first. It brought discoveries in science, art, politics, architecture, painting, music, literature, technology, and state & privately-funded explorations of distant lands. The scholars employed the humanist method— a philosophy that emphasized the ability of humans to act on their own instead of relying on the words of God. This was a critical moment as humans started being up front & center of driving change instead of being just a cog in the pre-renaissance rigid and fatalistic worldview. Not only this, but the Renaissance also saw the discovery of new continents, the replacement of the Ptolemaic system with the Copernican system of astronomy, the high rise of commerce, and the decline of the feudal system. Jules Michelet defined the 16th-century Renaissance in France as *"A period in Europe's cultural history that represented a break from the Middle Ages, creating a modern understanding of humanity and its place in the world."*

The Classical Renaissance can be seen as a sequential journey of three stages. The final stage is the ushering of the Classical Renaissance. This three-stage journey shaped the Classical Renaissance, and a similar three-stage journey is afoot as we speak, with the final stage leading to a Digital Renaissance.

- **Stage 1: Ready Infrastructure** - From a timeline perspective, the Roman Empire (600 BC - 500 AD) and Middle Ages (500-1450 AD) precede the Classical Renaissance. The Roman Empire laid the foundation for many social, military, and political institutions across Europe and North Africa. Physical infrastructure comprising public baths, aqueducts, amphitheatres, and roads came into being. The Middle Ages saw the building of many European cathedrals in Roman style. The Gothic style of architecture came into being during this period. There was an explosion in written literature documented through manuscripts. This creation of infrastructure that allowed people to travel, meet, exchange ideas, and capture thoughts through writing was a critical stage leading to the Classical Renaissance.

Well, one can think of the internet as the backbone of the digital infrastructure around the corner, just like the network of roads built before the Classical Renaissance. The buildings that contributed to the housing & exchange of ideas prior to the Classical Renaissance could be compared to server farms & cloud technology that holds today's digital information. Yes, just as physical infrastructure was in place before the Classical Renaissance, digital infrastructure is now in place before the Digital Renaissance is ushered in.

- **Stage 2: A Rude Shock** - During the Middle Ages, though the Europeans made advances in science and art, some rude shocks shook the population. Due to the unfortunate events of famine & Black Death, the Middle Ages are also called the "Dark Ages." When the Black Death swayed through Europe in 1347, it was one of the deadliest outbreaks in human history, wiping out one-third of the European population. During the famine, no social class, religion, or age group escaped the ravages. Fish and meat became scarce, and the fishing industry in Holland was affected by the trade imbalance due to the famine. Several diseases began to kill the cattle in

England that had survived the famine. The toll on human lives affected the wealthy as well as the underprivileged. Even the monasteries and convents were involved. It is hypothesized that the death and suffering in the aftermath of the Black Death galvanized the survivors to move ahead. It was a rude awakening of sorts., following a catastrophe. Curiosity and entrepreneurship grew manifold. It was as if the world moved a step back before moving two steps forward.

Covid was a rude shock to mankind in 2020. Who would have imagined that the entire world would be brought to a standstill despite so many advances on the scientific front? Covid was a rude shock for us in today's age. Digitalization got a bigger impetus during and in the aftermath of Covid. We are witnessing a new wave of curiosity and entrepreneurship. Maybe this rude awakening will help usher us into the Digital Renaissance.

- **Stage 3: Classical Renaissance** - The Classical Renaissance ushered in great advances in learning, secularism, rationality, logic, literature, art & humanism. But what transpired during this golden period of human history? Well, it was an all-around development across many disciplines with a lot of connecting the dots.

  o **First,** artists like Leonardo da Vinci incorporated scientific principles, such as human anatomy, into their work to recreate the human body through sculptures & paintings with extraordinary precision. Some of the most famous artistic works that were produced during the Renaissance include The Mona Lisa & The Last

Supper by Leonardo Da Vinci, The Statue of David & The Creation of Adam by Michelangelo. It also led to various scientific discoveries— Galileo and Descartes presented a new view of Astronomy and Mathematics. At the same time, Copernicus proposed that the sun was the center of the solar system and not the earth.

o **Second**, the Classical Renaissance led to the exploration of the physical world. While many Europeans pursued their ideals through art, literature, math, and science, others decided to sail and explore the world. Several voyagers, like Columbus, Ferdinand Magellan, Vasco De Gama, Marco Polo, and Hernan Cortes, launched expeditions to travel the globe. They discovered new shipping routes to America, India, and various other places. This is precisely why the Renaissance is sometimes called "The Age of Discovery." As we know, the invention of the Mariner's compass during the Classical Renaissance posed an impetus to navigation and paved the way for the process of colonization.

o **Third**, the Classical Renaissance was supported by rich merchants (akin to private equity investors of today) like the Medici family, also known as the House of Medici. The Medici family attained wealth and political power in Florence, Italy, roughly in the 13th century. The Medici story began when their family members from the Tuscan village of Cafaggiolo migrated to Florence. The Medicis rose to become one of the most important families in Florence through banking and commerce. Although the Medicis were a banking family from humble origins, they became one of the most powerful families in Europe, especially during the first half of the fifteenth century. Their financial prowess soon shifted them towards politics, and they eventually positioned themselves into Italian royalty. The Medicis are known to be patrons of art, fostering Renaissance in the country and revolutionizing the banking system.

o **Finally**, the Classical Renaissance benefited from and was supported by the democratization of information like Gutenberg's printing press and the First World Atlas. The invention of the movable printer in Europe is credited to the German printer Johannes Gutenberg. Zacharias Janssen, an ingenious spectacle maker of the Renaissance period, discovered the first microscope in 1590. When news about microscopes unfurled throughout Europe, the concept was adopted by others, including astronomer, physicist, and engineer Galileo Galilei, in the early 17th century. Besides these, Hans Lippershey, another canny spectacle maker of the Renaissance era from Holland, invented the first telescope in 1608. Initially, Lippershey christened his device *"kijker"* meaning "looker/seeing things far away as if they were nearby."

The ready infrastructure and a rude awakening laid the foundation for the Classical Renaissance. This period ushered in a new era with the rise of the notion of 'Humanism'- Attaching importance to the essence of individualism. Among its many principles, humanism promoted the idea that humans are at the center of their own universe and should embrace human achievements in education, classical arts, literature, and science. Humanism is a progressive philosophy of life without theism or other supernatural beliefs. It affirms our ability and responsibility to lead ethical lives of personal fulfillment that aspire to the greater good. Humanism is a rational philosophy informed by science, inspired by art, and motivated by compassion. Robert Wilde makes a remark on Renaissance humanism— 'The evolution of Renaissance Humanism as a method of thinking'.... Attempts by man to master nature rather than develop religious piety.'

With the digital infrastructure in place and as we come out of a rude awakening post-Covid, we are on the threshold of ushering in the Digital Renaissance. With Generative AI, it is not just about humans. It is humans and artificial Intelligence. Digital Renaissance could bring about "HumAInism." Just as Humanism shaped the Classical Renaissance, HumAInism (the coming together of humans and AI) will shape the Digital Renaissance.

Today, we live in a nonlinear world. As you can see, we are in a good position to usher in the Digital Renaissance. Still, there is one key difference— At the heart of the Classical Renaissance, there was a concept of *Festina Lente* / make haste slowly— the motto of the Medicis.

Festina lente
(Make Haste Slowly)

Please refer to the anchor and dolphin symbol (the dolphin represents haste, and the anchor represents slowly). Activities should be performed with a proper balance of urgency and diligence. In the present world, nonlinearity can play havoc with our minds, and haste would take over rational thinking. What sets *Festina Lente* apart is it does not command us to forsake haste wholly. Instead, it recognizes that the opposite of haste— be it procrastination or over-preparation can be just as debilitating. Therefore, we need to keep a balance with thoughtful diligence.

Overall, the Digital Renaissance could be a time of great creativity, innovation, and collaboration, potentially transforming our world in profound ways. While the Classical Renaissance and Digital Renaissance are separated by centuries, they share several similarities in their focus on humanity, aesthetics, technology, and collaboration. As stated previously, the Classical Renaissance was an era of significant cultural, artistic, and scientific growth in Europe during the 14th century. In a similar notion, today's technology could fuel the Digital Renaissance using the human + AI confluence. However, we will have to learn to navigate our nonlinear world, harness the positives, and not fall prey to the negatives.

Let's see how to reap the benefits of the Digital Renaissance through adopting the DeSIRe framework.

The "DeSIRe" Framework

Dictionary meaning of the word 'Desire': a strong feeling of wanting to have something or wishing for something to happen.

I am sure you recall the scene from the movie Matrix (first part of the original trilogy), where the character Neo, played by Keanu Reeves, is given a choice right at the beginning: Does he want the red or the blue pill? The red and blue pills metaphorically represent the choice between being willing to learn a potentially life-changing truth or being content with the current reality. Needless to say, Neo chooses the red pill, and the franchise takes off.

Let me explain my point:

Imagine you have to make a choice, like choosing between the colors red and blue. Our response to the Digital Renaissance is also a choice where either we could get the most out of it or miss out on the opportunities it brings. You need to have a strong desire to get the most out of it. You must want to understand how to use these new technologies and make them work for you. You also need to be ready to let go of some old habits and be open to trying new ones. It's like deciding between red and blue, but in this case, it's about embracing and benefitting from the changes in the digital world.

Generative AI is changing how we interact with computers, algorithms, and devices. In fact, it's making these interactions feel more like how we talk to other people. Here's the thing: it's becoming so advanced that soon, you might not even be able to tell if you're talking to a real human or an AI-powered device. That's how close the resemblance is getting. This might raise some questions and concerns about the future of technology and communication.

As detailed in the earlier chapter, HumAInism could help us progress only if we embrace it with all its challenges and advantages. To be fair, just having the desire (although it is necessary) may not be adequate. The next four chapters will detail the DeSIRe framework, which could enable us to navigate the nonlinear world.

Here is the DeSIRe framework:

You can approach this framework in a couple of different ways. The first is a more linear approach, meaning you follow a specific order: Delink, Simplify, Invest, and Reskill. This approach is structured and methodical.

Delink > Simplify > Invest > Reskill

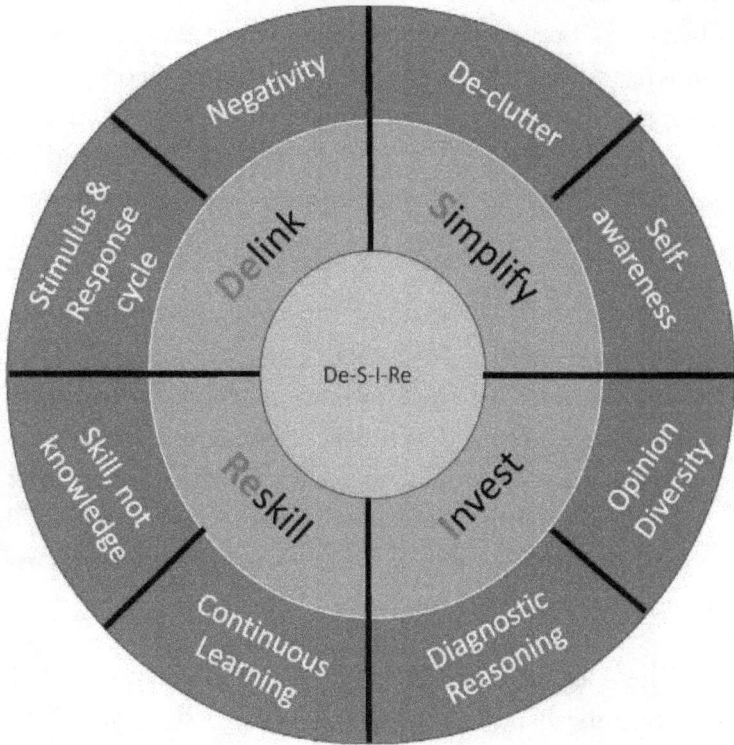

On the other hand, you can also choose to go through these steps in a more flexible, nonlinear way. This means you don't have to stick to a particular order. You can adapt the framework to your unique situation and preferences.

The choice is entirely up to you. You can follow the linear path or be creative and explore different orders. This flexibility allows you to tailor the framework to your specific needs and circumstances.

The next four chapters are organized in a linear way just for convenience and for maximum benefit. Here is what lies ahead:

In Chapter 5, we will closely examine the power of delinking in a world where we are 'Always On' or 'Always Connected' thanks to our devices and technology. We could benefit by understanding how the stimulus > response theory works and by adopting simple hacks to cultivate an informed and considered response to stimuli. This will help de-link ill-informed and non-considered responses from constant exposure to stimuli in this nonlinear connected world. We will also look at ways to delink ourselves from the negativity we always encounter in social media.

In Chapter 6, we will look at the power of simplification. Some simple steps and a little discipline could help us unlock two valuable weapons to take on the nonlinear world- time & focus. We will discuss the power of decluttering our minds through cultivating self-awareness. We will also delve into focussing on things that matter.

The elements of delinking & simplification will help in creating the bandwidth & motivation to slow ourselves down- akin to the anchor in *"Lente"* before we get ready to go fast- akin to the dolphin in *"Festina."*

Chapter 7 introduces the theme of 'investing'- investing time to be ready to benefit from the Digital Renaissance and investing in being exposed to and open to diverse opinions. We will discuss why exposing ourselves to diversity of opinions could help us think better and more effectively and avoid developing a narrow and biased worldview.

And finally, in Chapter 8, we look at the importance of re-skilling. The future will make different demands on us, and we must acquire tools and skills to prepare for it. We will look at some of the essential skills to navigate the increasingly nonlinear world. We would also examine why mere knowledge is not useful in the absence of skills to apply this knowledge. We will also delve into a framework to cultivate a continuous learning mindset.

The DeSIRe framework will be your guiding light as you get ready to navigate our increasingly nonlinear world and embrace the Digital Renaissance.

5

DELINK

"You have power over your mind – not outside events. Realize this, and you will find strength"
— *Marcus Aurelius*

Over the passage of time, psychologists and decision scientists have posed many theories regarding the manner in which we make decisions. Many of these theories attempt to establish the link between stimulus and response. However, only a few of them have tried to explain the impact of our response to a particular stimulus on how we learn over time. One such theory is the "Stimulus Response Theory of Learning," proposed by Edward Lee Thorndike, an American Psychologist who profoundly impacted behavior analysis and reinforcement theory.

When most people think about stimulus and response, Pavlov's conditioning experiment comes to their mind. In this famous experiment, the dog could be conditioned to give an answer (salivation) by associating a neutral stimulus (a ringing bell) with an unconditioned stimulus (food).

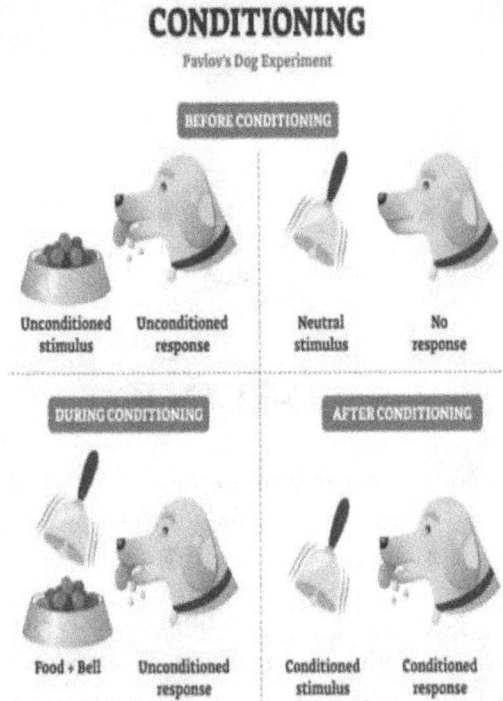

CONDITIONING
Pavlov's Dog Experiment

BEFORE CONDITIONING

| Unconditioned stimulus | Unconditioned response | Neutral stimulus | No response |

DURING CONDITIONING | AFTER CONDITIONING

| Food + Bell | Unconditioned response | Conditioned stimulus | Conditioned response |

Thorndike's approach was groundbreaking as it helped psychologists comprehend how animals and humans learn (beyond just conditioning) & how they can be adequately trained. Thorndike's theory proposes that all kinds of learning depend on the strength of the relationship between the stimulus & the response. In addition to this, new stimulus-response connections are strengthened only if a fulfilling result follows the response. For instance, Thorndike had placed a hungry cat in a puzzle box. There was only one outlet for the exit, which could be opened by correctly manipulating a latch. A fish was deliberately kept outside the box. The smell of the fish strongly motivated the hungry cat to come out of the box.

Consequently, the cat made every possible effort to free itself. The situation was described by Thorndike in 1911 as *"It tries to squeeze through every opening; it claws and bites at the bars or wires, it thrusts its paws through any opening and claws at everything it reaches."* In this manner, the cat attempted a series of random movements. In one of the random movements, the latch got manipulated by chance. The cat stormed out and got its reward responses. Now, it was able to open the door without any error. In other words, the cat learned how to open the door.

Edward Thorndike coined this notion as the 'stimulus-response' principle. According to this theory, the first requirement for learning is a 'stimulus,' and the second requirement is a 'response,' followed by the third requirement, which is a 'profound relationship between stimulus-response.' This principle is also called the 'contract-principle'. Over here, the learner reaches the correct response through random effort. Therefore, it is also called' the theory of trial and error.'

Interestingly, the relationship between the stimulus & response could lead to repeating or avoiding the answer based on whether it leads to satisfaction or dissatisfaction, which is precisely Thorndike's "Law of Effect," which suggests— *"Responses that produce a satisfying effect in a particular situation become more likely to occur again in that situation, and responses that produce a discomforting effect become less likely to occur again in that situation."* Therefore, the responses closely followed by satisfaction are undoubtedly to become firmly attached to the situation and more likely to re-establish when the situation is repeated. Conversely, suppose the situation is followed by discomfort and dissatisfaction. In that case, the connections to the situation will become fragile, and the response is less likely to occur when the situation is repeated. Let's say, for example— you arrive early to work consistently for a few days, and your boss praises your diligence. The praise and validation from your boss will likely make you feel good. Thus, you will be more drawn towards receiving that praise every day. Again, if you study hard and bear good fruit in your exam, you will likely double your efforts for the next exam and top the class. If you work diligently and do not receive a promotion or pay raise, you will be less satisfied with your organization and probably be compelled to leave.

Thorndike also proposed that the level of readiness impacts the strength of the relationship between stimulus and response, which is commonly termed Thorndike's "Law of Readiness." It is a psychological principle that explains how an individual's readiness to respond to a certain situation can influence their ability to learn and perform. According to Thorndike, learning usually occurs when an individual is prepared to learn/ put in effort, and the readiness to learn is determined by the person's experiences they faced in the past and the reinforcement they received for their actions. The law of readiness is closely linked to the concept of motivation. If an individual is motivated to learn and has an inherent desire to attain a particular goal, they are more likely to maximize their efforts and learn faster.

On the contrary, if individuals lack interest and motivation, they will barely have the patience to understand and learn anything. So, for example, if you are interested in understanding the gender oppression faced by women over the centuries, you are likely to read books by Simone De Beauvoir, Virginia Woolf,

Margaret Atwood, etc. Similarly, suppose you do not seek any interest in the concept of the multiverse. In that case, you are less likely to be interested in movies, comics, and documentaries that revolve around that particular theme.

From the above discussion, the key reader takeaway is that

Throndike's Stimulus Response Theory of Learning

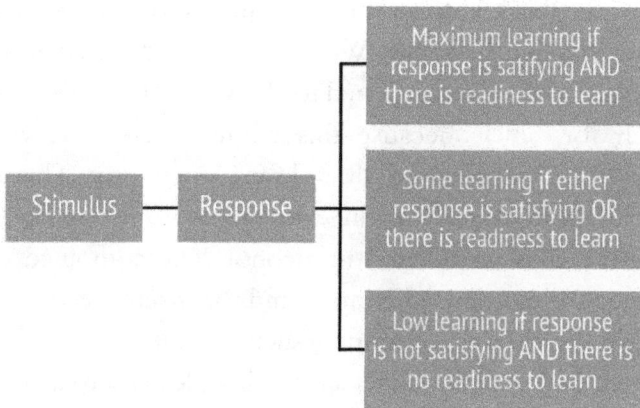

Stimulus — Response

Maximum learning if response is satifying AND there is readiness to learn

Some learning if either response is satisfying OR there is readiness to learn

Low learning if response is not satisfying AND there is no readiness to learn

response to a stimulus will keep recurring if the stimulus-response relationship is already strong & if the person is unwilling to re-evaluate or re-learn. When we learn something, such a strong relationship is already formed based on experience. This is how we all have learned- we respond to stimuli, and based on the reward or lack of it, this response may or may not be reinforced. Babies are naturally curious. They do what their instinct tells them to do. They need more patience, experience, or learning in the initial days. Over time, they will learn more from the 'stimulus-response leading to a reward' reinforcement route. However, for adults, the pace of new learning has already slowed due to learning over many years. Continuous repetition or avoidance will keep happening if you do not want to learn or delink from something you have learned in the past. On the other hand, considered or informed thinking could bring in new learning if there is a desire to do so. However, it requires cognitive effort and a desire to learn.

To my esteemed readers, the real question is— Why is the above understanding critical for the first step of delinking in the "DeSIRe" framework? Earlier in Chapter 1, we looked at the instant feedback loop as the consequence of the technology we are surrounded by today. We also discussed how social media, browsers, and apps are geared to show us content that we like or search for, solely because this content makes us visit these websites and apps repeatedly and for a longer time. This is almost akin to continuously giving directions to a liquor shop to someone who is addicted to alcohol. The combined effect of individually customized content and the instant feedback loop is that we increasingly encounter such stimuli (notifications, feeds that say 'you may like this') all the time, leading to a compulsive urge to respond, re-post, act upon, or share. This leads to a never-ending stimulus <-> response two-way loop (stimulus results in a response, but also the response leads to more such stimulation being shown to you) and is a vicious circle.

Stimulus <> response instant two-way loop

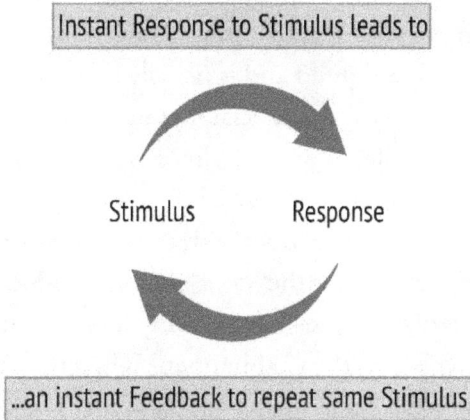

Instant Response to Stimulus leads to

Stimulus   Response

...an instant Feedback to repeat same Stimulus

Delinking comes to the rescue to break free from this vicious circle. However, before delving deep into how to delink, we must understand what happens when we succumb to the vicious stimulus <-> response loop. If we take a look at the work of behavioral economists Richard Thaler & Hers h Shefrin on the Dual Processing Model, we will realize that we are playing the role of a 'doer' most times and not a 'planner.' Thaler and Shefrin developed this model in their 1981 article, *"An economic theory of self-control,"* where they proposed two aspects of human nature.

Thaler & Shefrin state, *"The individual at any point in time is assumed to be both a farsighted planner and a myopic doer. The resulting conflict is seen to be fundamentally similar to the agency conflict between the owners and managers of a firm."* Their model was developed in the context of behaviors around financial savings, based on the concepts of a farsighted 'planner' and a short-sighted 'doer.' Based on their polarizing preferences, the planner and doer are in dire conflict with each other at any given time. The 'planner' is concerned with lifetime utility, so the 'planner' recognizes that every single decision should maximize utility.

On the other hand, the 'doer' only exists for fleeting moments and is selfish regarding those immediate desires. To sum it up, the 'planner' is foresighted and is usually in a position to consider the consequences of the decision and can make an optimal decision. Meanwhile, the 'doer' lives in the moment and goes with what appears right now. The 'planner' drives towards 'I should' thinking, but the 'doer' drives towards 'I want' thinking. The 'planner' can control the 'doer' through willpower. However, if any temptation comes along, the 'doer' can override the planner, which is exactly what happens when the vicious stimulus <-> response loop kicks in.

As already stated, the dual-self models in behavioral science refer to the conflict humans feel when trying to bridge the gap between their immediate desires and more beneficial options in the long run. While humans can sometimes be rational decision-makers who prioritize utility maximization, it does not always correspond to reality. For example, smokers make a conscious decision to enjoy the momentary dopamine hit from a cigarette over the long-term health benefits of avoiding tobacco, even if this behavior is not rational in any manner. Therefore, this model addresses the paradox created by classic economic views of decision utility by considering various decision criteria. Now, to give more control to the planner and not yield to being in a doer role all the time, we could do any of the three things below, which are key to delinking responses from stimuli:

- The **first** option is to create artificial hurdles or put restrictions such as archiving social media groups, disabling notifications or auto-downloads, and muting messages from social platforms.

- The **second** option is to create more decision points to force a 'pause and think' opportunity before auto-response occurs. For example, if we come across a post, it could help to research it, before forwarding it as is.

- The **third** option is to utilize the power of nudges to stop reverting to 'default': activating quiet time on the devices automatically, which is like having a new default. Browsing in incognito mode is another way to prevent reverting to default.

Therefore, we could attempt to break the vicious stimulus <-> response circle by using the above delinking techniques.

- **Firstly**, such techniques will encourage new learning by stopping 'revert to default' behavior.

- **Secondly**, forcing more system 2 thinking will increase our curiosity and openness to new learning.

Delinking is not just about delinking auto-default responses from the continuous stream of stimuli. The negativity coming through various stimuli must also be considered and delinked from. Research shows that social media evokes more polarized responses, especially the negative kind, and it is vital to protect oneself against such negativity. And this is where Stoicism comes to the rescue.

Stoicism was a school of Philosophy founded by Zeno of Athens in the 3rd century BC. It advocated achieving *eudaimonia* (happiness) through logic, which we can all benefit from in our quest to navigate the nonlinear world. Originally, Stoicism was known as Zenonism. However, the name was dropped in no time, as the Stoics did not consider their founders to be inherently wise and to avoid the risk of the philosophy becoming a cult of personality. It teaches the development of self-control and fortitude as a path to overcoming destructive emotions. The philosophy behind Stoicism holds the idea that becoming a clear and unbiased thinker allows one to understand the world even better. Stoicism suggests practicing self-control over excessive passion to overcome destructive emotions or negativity. The stoics believed that excess of good or bad passions drives negative emotions.

Interestingly, an excess of good passions could drive negative emotions, too! They believed that if we must not yield to excessive passion, we should not yield to passions that concern things outside our control. Thus, this is the concept of control—controlling the controllable and letting go of everything else.

As Epictetus says, "Some things are in our control and others not. Things in our control are opinion, pursuit, desire, aversion, and our own actions. Things not in our control are body, property, reputation, command, and whatever are not our own actions." The Roman Stoic Epictetus introduces the dichotomy of control at the beginning of his book *Enchiridion*. The Stoics believed that there were honestly only two things we had direct control over— our voluntary actions and how we think about things. Everything that exists—such as our bodily sensations, the past, other people's opinions about us, and the outcome of our actions— is outside and beyond our direct control. The crucial point is that we should adopt a rational attitude to things, depending on whether we can control them or not. Therefore, it is vital to focus on "controlling the controllable" and cultivate an attitude of detachment from everything else.

To sum up, we have learned that the process of delinking starts with an awareness of the stimuli around us and our responses to them. In order to escape the vicious circle of stimulus <-> response in this nonlinear world, we need to encourage the planner mindset or force system two thinking. If we create artificial hurdles, more decision points, or use the power of positive nudges, it could help break down the vicious circle of stimulus <-> response. The general understanding and practice of the Stoic principle of 'dichotomy of control' could help us control the negativity associated with our interactions with technology. Thus, delinking could help us break the vicious circle of stimulus <-> response, limiting the addictive & negative impact of today's technology and preparing us to embrace the positives provided by modern-day technology.

6

SIMPLIFY

"You Have So Many Goals You Never Finished, Dreams You Never Followed. You're Living Your Worst You."

- Alpha Waymond, Everything Everywhere All At Once

Alpha Waymond's dialogue from the Oscar-winning movie *Everything Everywhere All At Once* is full of emotion and symbolism. If you look closely, too many things are happening all at once in this nonlinear world— Have you ever thought about your daily schedule and realized that your life looks the same every day? Have you ever taken a walk down memory lane and envisioned that you are yet to achieve the goals you had planned years ago? Well, I am sure we all feel like hamsters on a wheel most of the time. There is a feeling that we are always running behind, time is ticking away quickly, and so many things are yet to be done. In the previous chapter, we delved into how the instant feedback loop in our nonlinear world and an overdose of stimuli lead to an incessant stimulus <-> response two-way vicious loop. However, there lies another fallout of this never-ending vicious circle. In general, we are just overwhelmed with what we need to finish in a typical day, with a sea of to-do lists, reminders, and alarms reminding us all the time about our inadequacies and unfinished work. We are almost trapped in the Sisyphean monotony of doom and boredom.

Modern day Sisyphus going through daily routine

Image by kjpargeter on Freepik

To my esteemed readers, tell me— Don't you wish at times that we should be able to let go of all these troubles and lead a worry-free life? Unfortunately, this seems like an uphill task in an always-on & always-connected nonlinear world and is easier said than done. The process of dealing with this feeling of being overwhelmed needs to start with us. The idea of self-awareness is critical to figure out the areas you can strive for better. In today's nonlinear world, our brains are under constant pressure to cope with the ongoing demands due to the stimulus <-> response loop. So, understanding how our brains function is an excellent first step towards self-awareness. According to the author Mark Manson, self-awareness can be understood on various levels. On the surface, it indicates being conscious of your actions. At a deeper level, it means recognizing the issues you create for yourself and finding solutions to fix them.

The term "Temet Nosce" or "know thyself" is a philosophical maxim inscribed upon the Temple of Apollo in the ancient Greek precinct of Delphi. Ion of Chios, a Greek philosopher, made an explicit allusion to the proverb— The principal meaning of the phrase was "know your limits," either in the sense of knowing the extent of one's abilities, knowing one's place in the social scale, or knowing oneself to be mortal. In the 4th century BC, the maxim was drastically re-interpreted by Plato, who understood it to mean, broadly speaking, "know your soul." If you are a Keanu Reeves fan and have had the opportunity to follow the Matrix series, then I'm sure you have come across the phrase "Temet Nosce," which was on a sign above Oracle's (Gloria Foster) kitchen door. Also, the company Neo (Keanu Reeves) worked for was called MetaCortex. This word means "transcending the limits of one's mind" or "liberating one's mind," which Neo eventually did quite successfully, if I may add.

In the early days of computing, our brain was considered to be similar to what a computer was meant to be. Isn't our brain supposed to gather information using various senses like a computer receiving inputs through a keyboard, camera, or microphone? Isn't it then supposed to process the information and finally store it like a computer? Although there is agreement that our biological brains create our conscious minds, there needs to be more clarity on the role played regarding information processing - the crucial similarity that brains and computers are presumed to share. Since we discovered that machines could solve problems by manipulating symbols, we have wondered if the brain might work similarly. Alan Turing predicted that by 2000, "*One will be able to speak of machines thinking without expecting to be contradicted.*" If machines could think like humans, it was natural to wonder if brains might work like machines.

One might even think, "The computer has bytes and the brain has neurons. How do we compare the two?" The difference between the human brain and the computer is the ability of neurons to combine to assist with creating and storing memories. Each neuron has thousands of connections to other neurons. With over a trillion connections in an average human brain, this overlap effect creates an exponentially massive linkage capacity.

If you look at it minutely with a clear perspective, human beings, and computers have their strengths based on what one is looking for. A computer is the clear choice if you want precision and raw processing speed. On the other hand, if you want creativity, energy efficiency, and empathy, the human mind is your best bet. Today, we live in a world where computers can outperform humans at several things. Artificial intelligence and machine learning will lead to new breakthroughs, leaving us wondering whether we shall soon live in a technological utopia or battle for survival against a cyborg version of Arnold Schwarzenegger. Blake Richards, a neuroscientist and computer scientist at McGill University in Montreal, says, "*Brains process*

everything in parallel, in continuous time rather than in discrete intervals."
Even Michael Graziano, a neuroscientist at Princeton University,
believes that *"There's a broader concept of what a computer is, as a thing
that takes in information and manipulates it and, on that basis, chooses
outputs. And a 'computer' in this more general conception is what the brain
is; that's what it does."*

But in many respects, our brains are very different from how
computers function. Dr. Thomas K Landauer, a cognitive
scientist, had challenged this "brain-as-a-computer" thinking. He
estimated the storage size required to store an average adult's
knowledge. For example, how much storage is needed to store
an average adult's vocabulary of a few thousand words? Through
extrapolations, Dr. Landeaur estimated the available storage
space of a human brain to be around 1 GB, which is virtually
nothing compared to the storage space of computers and servers
we use.

In comparison, even a basic smartphone has 64-516 GB of
storage space, which can be easily enhanced by attaching a
memory card. Landauer's work established that our brains are
not meant to store vast amounts of data, unlike computers. They
are akin to diagnostic reasoning machines that continuously look
at our past beliefs, factor in recent experiences, and try to make
sense of the future in our complex world. The 'planner' and
'doer' roles exist in harmony. Our brains are wired to call upon
the right role depending on the task.

We know that computers are very accurate and swift at simple
math, and if users can break complex math into simple
components, computers can be just as accurate and as fast at very
complex math as well. However, much of what humans use their
brains for has yet to be broken down structurally and imitated by

computers. At the core of Thomas Landauer's argument is a criticism of how organizations are run, and it is a criticism that Shoshanna Zuboff registered in *In the Age of the Smart Machine* in 1988. Like Zuboff, Landauer agrees that too many organizations use modern technology to apply the principle of the division of labor to brainwork. In this process, exciting jobs turn into boring ones, damage employee morale and interest in work, and miss myriad opportunities for the enhancement of productivity.

When we become self-aware, we tend to focus on things that matter instead of worrying about everything that comes our way. It helps in decluttering. Self-awareness also helps us sharpen our diagnostic reasoning skills, that make us uniquely human. Psychologists Shelley Duval & Robert Wicklund proposed the idea that: *"Self-awareness is the ability to focus on yourself and how your actions, thoughts, or emotions do or don't align with your internal standards. If you are highly self-aware, you can objectively evaluate yourself, manage your emotions, align your behavior with your values, and understand correctly how others perceive you."*

Simply put, individuals with a high level of self-awareness can interpret their actions, feelings, and thoughts more objectively than those without self-awareness. Developing self-awareness is essential as it allows leaders to assess their growth effectiveness and change course when necessary. When we look outwardly, we understand how people perceive us.

People who are aware of how people see them are more likely to be empathetic and compassionate to others with different perspectives. Finally, and most importantly, self-awareness could make us worry less. For example, Rudolf Abel's character is accused of spying in the movie Bridge of Spies, produced by Steven Speilberg. Instead of panicking, he maintains his composure so well that his lawyer, James Donovan, asks him why he is not alarmed. Rudolf Abel replies, saying, "Would it help?" Once you are truly aware of who you are and what you want, you can turn any situation in your favor. You will be able to maintain your calm and see things through a rational perspective instead of an emotional or ignorant one. If you are familiar with the widely celebrated show Game of Thrones, I am sure you have come across the quick-witted character Tyrion Lannister, who rightly says, *"Never forget what you are, the rest of the world will not. Wear it like armor and it can never be used to hurt you."*

So, how do we develop self-awareness and 'Simplify' our lives?

- **First**, by making time for self-reflection and being mindful— Blocking time can be a vital way to ensure that you make time for self-reflection, especially when you feel like you are too busy. The American Psychological Association describes self-reflection as "the examination, contemplation, and analysis of one's thoughts, feelings, and actions," psychologists describe "self-reflective awareness" as one of the most crucial life skills a person can have. You can reflect on the 'self' by playing soothing music, walking, practicing meditation, etc. When practicing self-reflection, see and decide what feels most comfortable for your body, whether walking, dancing, sitting cross-legged, or lying down. Choosing the correct posture helps in eliminating stress. Most importantly, be kind to yourself. You should sit down and reflect on your positive and negative emotions, fears, and strengths and face them. Practicing mindfulness will likely create space and time to connect with your inner self and carve out solitude.

- **Second**, by actively listening to yourself and others— Active listening is a communication skill that involves going beyond simply hearing the words being uttered by another person but also seeking to understand the meaning and intent behind them. It requires being an active participant in the process of communication. If you want to get involved in proper conversations, listening with your full attention helps you understand the topic better. When you practice active listening, you are fully engaged and immersed in what the other person is trying to convey. To be an active listener, put away your cell phone, ignore distractions/notifications, and avoid daydreaming. Active listening refers to paying attention to the explicit and implicit information you receive in a conversation. Nonverbal cues, such as tone of voice, facial expression, and body language, are usually where the motivation and emotion behind the words are expressed. Let the other person speak their mind so you can hear their perspective. Even if you do not fully agree with them, do not let your prejudices get in the way of their opinions. Please keep an open mind and try to picture things from their point of view instead of asserting dominance.

- **Last**, by journaling daily— In today's fast-paced world, it is natural for any individual to feel overwhelmed, stressed, or disconnected from their inner selves. By expressing one's thoughts and feelings in a journal, we can gain clarity, insight, and perspective on our lives and develop a more positive, resilient, and mature mindset. Some of history's greatest thinkers believed journaling benefits mental clarity, personal growth, and creative expression. Scientists and artists like Albert Einstein, Leonardo da Vinci, Frida Kahlo, Franz Kafka, Vincent Van Gogh, and Marie Curie recorded their ideas, insights, and personal struggles through journaling. Maintaining a journal is a self-care practice that can powerfully impact your well-being. Negative emotions can often dominate our thoughts and create mood swings. Instead of bottling up feelings of anger, frustration, or disappointment, you can write about them in a journal. The art of journaling provides stress relief, and penning things down can also help you process and figure out solutions to problems. Journaling is a way to help us navigate these challenges and cultivate a more profound sense of self-awareness, mindfulness, and creativity.

It is important to note that journaling differs from the 'To-Do' lists that most of us create daily. The 'To-Do' list consists of simple tasks. On the other hand, journalism focuses more on capturing our experiences, struggles, and learnings every day. The author Daniel Markovitz says, *"Stop making 'To-Do' lists. They're simply setting you up for failure and frustration."*

If you love using 'To-Do' lists to organize your tasks and can't imagine your life without them, you might find inspiration in the 'To-Do' lists of Leonardo da Vinci, a famous figure often referred to as the Renaissance man. Leonardo da Vinci was known for his incredible talents and diverse interests, from art to science.

The idea here is that Leonardo's 'To-Do' lists can be a great source of inspiration for your own 'To-Do' lists. He was an avid learner and believed in focusing on tasks that truly mattered. By examining his lists, you can see how he managed his time and channeled his efforts into continuous learning and activities that had a significant impact.

Leonardo da Vinci's To-Do List

SOURCE https://www.npr.org/sections/krulwich/2011/11/18/142467882/leonardos-to-do-list

- GET THE MASTER OF ARITHMATIC TO SHOW YOU HOW TO SQUARE A TRIANGLE
- DRAW MILAN
- EXAMINE THE CROSSBOW OF MAESTRO GIANETTO
- GET MESSEA FAZIO TO SHOW YOU ABOUT PROPORTION OF HUMAN BODY
- DISCOVER THE MEASUREMENT OF THE CASTELLO (THE DUKE'S PALACE)
- CALCULATE THE MEASUREMENT OF MILAN AND SUBURBS
- ASK ABOUT THE MEASUREMENT OF THE SUN, PROMISED ME BY MAESTRO GIOVANNI FRANCESE

Seeking inspiration from Leonardo's *To-Do'lists* can help you structure your tasks in a way that promotes lifelong learning and prioritizes the most important and meaningful activities in your life. It's a way to approach your 'To-Do' lists with the mindset of a true Renaissance person like Leonardo da Vinci.

Thus, we learned from this chapter that simplification starts with self-awareness. When we see ourselves clearly, we become more confident and creative. We make wise decisions, build stronger relationships, and communicate more effectively. We become less likely to deviate from our goals. We become better workers and influential leaders with a zeal. The better we understand ourselves, the better we get at dealing with the nonlinear world. The power of self-reflection or being mindful is invaluable. When we practice focusing our attention on the present moment, it becomes a critical element of stress reduction and improves overall well-being.

Practicing mindfulness makes you less likely to be wired up about the future. Being mindful makes it convenient to *seize the day* and savor the pleasures in life as they occur and creates a greater capacity to deal with times of adversity. Instead of overloading our brains or doing endless multi-tasking, we should hone our diagnostic reasoning skills and focus on things that matter. Lastly, journaling is a good way to reflect and force us to use diagnostic reasoning. It creates a safe space for everyone to express personal impressions, daily experiences, evolving insights, dreams, and creative musings. Delinking and Simplification are the first steps on the journey toward Digital Renaissance. The time and energy you will save through these two steps could be invested for personal progress. We will discuss this in the next chapter.

7

INVEST

"Curiosity is the wick in the candle of learning"

— William Arthur Ward

Before we delve into this chapter, let us take a moment to ponder on something interesting. I know this may seem totally out of the blue, but has it ever occurred to you how incredible octopuses are? They have eight tentacles and a large brain relative to their body mass. In fact, they have the most significant brain-to-body ratio among all invertebrates. Octopuses are known to be intelligent. They can build small structures by piling rocks, broken shells, broken glass, etc. They possess a unique camouflaging ability & can easily change color to merge with their environment. To delve deeper— They have three hearts. One heart circulates blood around the body, and the other two pump blood past its gills to pick up oxygen. Their blood is blue, and their brain is shaped like a doughnut. In addition to the above-stated facts, each of their eight arms has a mini-brain that allows them to move their long arms quickly and instantaneously, which also means that octopuses can taste with each of their arms. Most importantly, they use water jet propulsion to propagate through water.

You must be wondering why this chapter details the remarkable qualities of an octopus. Well, this book is not a treatise on octopuses for sure, but just for a moment- imagine living the life of an octopus for a day or being blessed with octopus-like features for a day. Tell me, would it not be wonderful if our hands had their own mini-brains and if they could function independently of each other? In that case, our multi-tasking ability will go up multiple folds. Imagine if we had two hearts— one to pump blood throughout the body and another exclusively for our lungs. Would that make us run faster without feeling tired? Well, maybe organizations could adopt a more agile and decentralized leadership model inspired by multiple brains and arms of the octopus.

In the previous chapter, we briefly touched upon the concept of diagnostic reasoning. Diagnostic reasoning has its roots in medical science. According to NIH, "*Diagnostic reasoning is a dynamic thinking process that leads to the identification of a hypothesis that best explains the clinical evidence.*" Diagnosis is the art of determining a disease by an individual's signs, symptoms, and test results. The word "Diagnosis" comes from the Greek word "*diagignoskein,*" which means to distinguish or to discern. Identifying or determining a patient's underlying illness is critical to being an effective doctor. However, diagnostic reasoning and diagnostic decision-making are critical not only for healthcare professionals.

The concept of diagnostic reasoning is equally applicable in real life. Diagnostic reasoning forces us to take the planner role and makes us avoid herd mentality. The exercise to imagine the life of an octopus or, for that matter, anything or everything in Leonardo De Vinci's lists, is an exercise in diagnostic reasoning that pushes us to think instead of unquestioningly accepting things as they are. Diagnostic reasoning is a critical skill in navigating the nonlinear world. One must always remember technology will make things very easy for us through spoon-feeding, so we must consciously wean ourselves away from any false sense of comfort. If we do not force ourselves to practice diagnostic reasoning, our fate will be similar to that of the people in Plato's cave.

An Illustration of The Allegory of the Cave, from Plato's Republic

In the Allegory of the Cave, presented by the Greek philosopher Plato, in his epic *Republic*— he describes a group of cave people who have lived all their lives being chained to the wall of a cave, facing a blank wall where they see shadows of actual objects. For cave people, shadows constitute reality since they do not realize that what they see are mere shadows of objects in front of a fire, much less that these objects are inspired by actual things outside the cave that they cannot perceive. Through this allegory, Plato attempts to differentiate between what we perceive and what may be accurate. This is where diagnostic reasoning comes into play. Plato's disciple, Socrates, further explains how a philosopher is like a prisoner freed from Plato's cave and comes to understand that the shadows on the wall are not the direct source of the images seen. A philosopher aims to understand and perceive the higher levels of reality.

In contrast, the other inmates of the cave do not even desire to leave their prison, for they know no better life. Socrates believed the shadows were the ultimate reality for the prisoners since they had never seen anything else. Needless to say, all of us may not be interested in becoming a philosopher, but the conscious practice of diagnostic reasoning could certainly help us appreciate and understand our nonlinear world.

There are three steps to developing diagnostic reasoning:

(1) **Investing time in running What-If scenarios -** An overdose of stimuli characterizes ou r nonlinear world. This overdose interferes with our reasoning ability by overwhelming us. Investing time in running What-If scenarios helps in restoring reasoning abilities. Here is a simple example of cultivating diagnostic reasoning through running

such What-If scenarios. All of us learn history in school. We remember the dates of various battles—when this battle was fought, where it was fought, and who won, but do we push ourselves to think about what would have happened if the outcome were to be different? What would the rewritten European history be like if Napoleon did not lose the battle of Waterloo? Would inflation still have been a big issue in 2022-23 if the Russia - Ukraine crisis had not occurred at the beginning of 2022?

Obviously, there are no correct answers to running these "what-if" scenarios. Rather, the main objective is to force ourselves to think and imagine multiple possibilities. This process will help in sharpening our diagnostic reasoning abilities over time. Imagine if we could run one such what-if scenario in our minds every day for just ten minutes. This habit could build an invaluable treasure of well-thought-out opinions and perspectives to help us navigate the nonlinear world more confidently.

(2) **Investing time in seeking, evaluating, and integrating diverse opinions** is equally critical in developing diagnostic reasoning. Through the lenses of race, ethnicity, ability, gender, and beyond, diversity can help build a balanced perspective. Previously, we have discussed how social media leads to polarization. Several people argue that we increasingly live in an online filter bubble that only exposes us to the ideas we previously agreed with. The nonlinear world makes it easier for us to listen

to groups or individuals who validate our own perspectives. Actively seeking diverse opinions is an excellent way to counter this biased thinking.

In his book *The Opposable Mind: How Successful Leaders Win Through Integrative Thinking*, Roger Martin emphasizes the importance of integrative thinking. He defines integrative thinking as "The ability to face the tension of opposing ideas constructively and, instead of choosing one at the expense of the other, generate a creative resolution of the tension in the form of a new idea that contains elements of the opposing ideas but is superior to each." Martin states that, as opposed to conventional thinkers, integrative thinkers take a magnanimous view of what is salient despite the increase in the complexity of problems. They consider multi-directional and nonlinear causal relationships and keep the entire situation in mind while working on individual segments and searching for creative resolutions. Come to think of it- humans are one of the few species blessed with opposable thumbs. An opposable thumb refers to the position and movement of the thumb, which is in the opposite direction as the rest of the fingers. This allows us to have a solid grip and lift things. An opposable mind, in a metaphorical way, shares a similar trait. It is able to argue for and against, hold opposite thoughts simultaneously, and have a solid grip on any situation. Given the instant feedback loop and always-on nature of connectedness, our nonlinear world forces us to take sides instantaneously. There is never time to evaluate, verify, or make an informed decision. However, seeking diverse opinions by cultivating an opposable mind facilitates integrative thinking.

(3) **Holding opinions without passion:** The Philosopher Bertrand Russel mentioned, *"When there are rational grounds for an opinion, people are content to set them forth and wait for them to operate. In such cases, people do not passionately hold their opinions; they hold them calmly and set forth their reasons quietly. The opinions that are held with passion are always those for which no good ground exists; indeed passion is the measure of the holder's lack of rational conviction. Opinions in politics and religion are almost always held passionately."* In today's trigger-happy, always-on world, most people gravitate towards simpler solutions without defining or understanding the problem or issue at hand. Albert Einstein said, *"I usually spend 99% of time defining the problem, and the remaining 1% on the solution."* Even Abraham Lincoln stated, *"If you give me 6 hours to chop down a tree, I will spend the first four sharpening the ax."* Social media, in particular, and our nonlinear world, in general, are characterized by this unfortunate truth- when it comes to expressing an opinion, the speed and emotional intensity overshadow the quality and soundness of that opinion. You just have to look around. Look at any online news article and the comments below it. No matter what the article is all about, many people will always find a way to link the article to a political party or religion they strongly believe in or against! The key to fighting polarization

and the resultant groupthink is cultivating the habit of forming and discussing opinions without passion.

In the earlier two chapters, we saw that De-linking and Simplification are critical stages of developing focus and freeing up time. Investing the freed-up time in developing diagnostic reasoning can yield rich dividends while navigating our nonlinear world. Running What-If scenarios, encouraging diversity of opinions leading up to integrative thinking, and cultivating the habit of holding opposing opinions in a dispassionate way are good practices to take on the nonlinear world. For sure, a lot of this requires not only a desire to do so and invest time, but one also needs to be sensitive to developing newer skills and adapting to the nonlinear world that requires us to learn continuously. We will discuss this in the next chapter.

8

RESKILL

"The main lesson of thirty-five years of AI research is that the hard problems are easy and the easy problems are hard. . . . As the new generation of intelligent devices appears, it will be the stock analysts and petrochemical engineers and parole board members who are in danger of being replaced by machines. The gardeners, receptionists, and cooks are secure in their jobs for decades to come."

- Erik Brynjolfsson, The Second Machine Age: Work, Progress, and Prosperity in a Time of Brilliant Technologies

All right, folks, I have an intriguing question for you. Have you ever wondered what these intriguing-sounding people did for a living: a gong farmer, a film boxer, a powder monkey, a lector, a Dictaphone operator, or the typing pool ladies?

These job titles may sound like something out of a bygone era, and you might be scratching your head trying to figure them out in today's world. However, each of these roles represented a legitimate profession during their respective time periods. People used to make their livelihoods by working in these positions.

Let us take the example of a gong farmer to give you a glimpse into this historical job jargon. In the 18th century in England, a gong farmer was a person responsible for the rather unenviable task of digging out and removing human excrement from cesspits. It is a stark reminder of how professions have evolved over time, and what was once a common occupation might seem unusual or even unfathomable in today's context.

If you take a walk down the labyrinth of history— during the chronology of humanity, old jobs have disappeared, and new ones have come up. Today, it is difficult to imagine 'being a farmer' as a new job, but when our hunter-gatherer ancestors started settling down, farming was a new job. Doctors and engineers were unknown professions a few centuries ago. While technology has added countless jobs to the workforce over the past century, it has also made a host of occupations obsolete along the way. Well, this is how the old gives way to the new. This is what we precisely call life. Several occupations that were commonplace in the past no longer exist on resumes today and are not in demand. They are no longer seen as valuable or even remotely important to any extent. Some of the jobs disappeared due to the advancement of technology, while others were intentionally replaced due to improved labor laws.

In a similar manner, AI threatening jobs should not make front-page news. After all, mechanization has made many human effort-led tasks redundant. Automation has not been invented today! Machines have been replacing manual labor at a gradual rate ever since the dawn of the Industrial Revolution. It started with agriculture and skilled crafts like hand weaving, mass manufacturing, and other repetitive clerical tasks. It is not surprising that with AI, too, there are numerous reports about jobs getting eliminated due to these new-age algorithms. Yoshua Bengio, a professor and Artificial Intelligence researcher at the University of Montreal, says, *"Today's systems are not anywhere close to posing an existential risk. But in one, two, five years? There is too much uncertainty. That is the issue. We are not sure this won't pass some point where things get catastrophic."*

The work done by Carl Frey & Michael Osborne rang the first alarm bells in 2013 when they concluded that 47% of jobs could be automated in a decade due to technology-led automation, based on extensive analysis of the extent of automation possible as well as the degree of criticality of various jobs. Digital/AI technology is set to cause more upheaval than earlier technologies because changes are occurring more rapidly than ever before. AI fundamentally alters how we live, function, work, and, more importantly, think, communicate, and learn. Modern-day AI technology is enabling not just the automation of repetitive tasks but also some cognitive tasks. As we have seen earlier, most of yesteryear's technologies have reduced physical efforts. Today, technology reduces mental efforts and enables algorithms, AI agents, and computers to read emotions, create music, or speak like humans. Today's technology has the potential to challenge what is unique to humans.

We will not be wrong to conclude that we are on the verge of a second Cambrian explosion. The original Cambrian explosion occurred more than 500 million years ago. This was when most major groups of animals first appeared on Earth within a relatively short period. It was when life was created on Earth. This groundbreaking event lasted for nearly 13 to 25 million years and resulted in the emergence of most animal species. The Cambrian explosion fuelled a world filled with complex lifeforms with anatomical features that we witness in modern animals.

Why would one think we are on the verge of a second Cambrian explosion? According to Yuval Noah Harari, a professor in the Department of History at the Hebrew University of Jerusalem, *"AI has hacked the operating system of our civilization."* It is believed that language, cultural codes/artifacts that we all jointly believe in (our legal system, money, and democracy...to name a few) & the art of storytelling makes us human. It is the first time in our history that a non-human (Generative AI agent) may be as good as, if not better, in this. Money, religion, and democracy are all human-created artifacts. It may be a matter of time before Generative AI starts influencing the next religion or the next forthcoming political system. As we are currently in the fourth epoch of technology adoption, the question of how work is being redefined is something that many look forward to unraveling, especially with the advent of Generative AI like ChatGPT.

The fear of AI taking over humanity has haunted mankind for some time, especially through popular Science Fiction. These fears mainly focused on machines using their will, intelligence, and superlative physical means to kill, enslave, or subjugate people. But over the past few decades, many new advances in AI have emerged that threaten the survival of human civilization from an unanticipated direction. If an AI agent is indistinguishable from another human in a virtual world, the threat comes from within and is challenging to identify. The danger is not about a super robot trying to take over the world, but about an AI agent indistinguishable from a human being manipulating human opinion or actions.

This may sound rather bleak, but I believe governments and corporations will come together to implement some safeguards. At a general level, everyone's concern should have more to do with humanity's inability to cope with the changed reality. Sydney Harris says, *"The real danger is not that computers will begin to think like men, but that men will begin to think like computers."* The benefits far outweigh the risks as long as we have some safeguards to encourage responsible AI usage. For example, a car helps us reach our destination from point A to point B faster than walking for hours. Over the past few decades, cars have improved their durability and safety. However, several accidents still occur, and numerous lives are lost daily, with driver faults being the main reason for these accidents. This does not make automotive technology intrinsically bad. It pushes us to increase the safety threshold and put forth stricter laws to reduce the risks... The same idea applies to any technology, notably AI. If technology is misused, it will backfire on us. Around 1.1 billion jobs will be radically transformed by technology over the next decade. Is this the end of the road for humans? Well, we need to not only step up but also evolve consistently.

Elbert Hubbard says, *"One machine can do the work of fifty ordinary men. No machine can do the work of one extraordinary man."* With Generative AI, we are entering an era where progress could be limited not by technology but by our imagination. Erik Brynjolfsson says, *"There is no better resource for improving the world and bettering the state of humanity than the world's humans—all 7.1 billion of us.* " To cope with the rampant digitalization, every individual needs to hone a few skills instead of acquiring just academic or bookish knowledge. In fact, by dedicating yourself to learning valuable skills, you can find greater opportunities for personal and professional triumphs. A leading AI scientist and researcher rightly states, *"Stop learning tasks, start learning skills."*

The first step towards reskilling ourselves in order to navigate our nonlinear world is to differentiate between knowledge and skills. According to the Oxford Dictionary, knowledge comprises facts acquired through experience or education. In today's world, knowledge is largely democratized with Google Search, Wikipedia, YouTube, ChatGPT, and multiple such avenues to get information. To survive in today's world, only knowledge will not suffice. Let's take an example to illustrate this point: many people do not know how a bicycle works. In fact, even fewer people will know how a car works. But does this lack of knowledge hinder us from riding a bicycle or driving a car? Not really. In today's world, skills are more important than knowledge.

In the world of Generative AI and in an era where computers & algorithms are becoming human-like, three types of skills will be increasingly valued:

1) **Creator skills**: One must use the power of technology to create the new and change the old. Repetitive tasks will be automated- no doubt about that! Albert Einstein said, "The world as we have created it, is a result of our thinking. It cannot be changed without changing our thinking." In the process of learning and building skills, our thinking plays a vital role. The approach we use to solve a

problem or implement a plan or strategy begins with our process of thinking. There are basically two contrasting ways of thinking— linear & nonlinear.

On the one hand, linear thinking is structured, process-oriented, and sequential. Most of our formal education systems encourage structured thinking. When a novice student with minimal knowledge starts learning from scratch, linear or structured thinking is essential. But as we saw earlier, knowledge is getting democratized in today's world, and what you do with the knowledge and how you are able to apply this knowledge is important. Adopting nonlinear thinking comes in handy here. Nonlinear thinking is more abstract in nature and characterized by the ability to create connections between ideas, even when they are not completely related. Leonardo de Vinci - our original Renaissance man - demonstrated this well during the Classical Renaissance period. Nonlinear thinking is more creative and relies on experience, intuition, and imagination to understand problems and to brainstorm alternate solutions. Earlier chapters discussed how investing time in honing our diagnostic reasoning ability is critical in our nonlinear world. This could form a strong base to build creative skills. Today's world provides opportunities for anyone and everyone to be a creator or an influencer. Today's world favors technological 'hacks' over theoretical knowledge. Thousands of people are making a living by being creators in today's economy. New skills such as prompt creation and prompt engineering will be in demand in the future for better human-AI agent interfaces.

2) **Co-curation**: Humans are good at learning from experiences. The power of curating helps us to leverage these experiences and expertise accumulated over time. It is as if we all have an individual in-built foundation model within us that has been continuously trained since we were born. Generative AI is taking baby steps in this respect right now. Linear thinking may not help you cope with a nonlinear world. Instead of focusing on sequential, structured ways, nonlinear thinking focuses on connecting the dots.

Interestingly, Generative AI could be an ally in this regard. The combination of AI+human (we talked about HumAInism in one of the earlier chapters) is more potent than ever than what humans or Generative AI could do individually. Going ahead, it won't be just about human curation. Human + AI co-creation will be the game changer. Leveraging the generative abilities of AI could leapfrog the curation process to a degree not yet seen. Even now, people are co-curating art, music, or even literature without being programmers or coders.

3) **Collaborate**: The collective wisdom of humanity has got us here, and there is no reason to believe that it can't take us forward in an increasingly nonlinear world. We need to collaborate with each other even more. Nonlinear thinking involves embracing uncertainty, taking an integrative approach to

problem-solving, and seeing connections and patterns that are not immediately obvious. Today's technology makes it much easier to collaborate than ever before. We don't need to be physically together to collaborate. Experience with remote working during the recent Covid pandemic has shown us that. Digital collaboration is also a great leveler- it is easy to talk to people anytime from any part of the world and work together. Recent focus on inclusion and diversity in offices, schools, and society makes collaboration even more productive. Cloud computing and an upsurge in collaborative platforms have made collaboration easy.

Given the pace and nonlinearity of change, the above-mentioned skills cannot be acquired as a one-time acquisition. The ultimate objective is to go on a journey of continuous learning. The world that we live in is dynamic and rapidly evolving, and continuous learning will be an indispensable tool for every individual. Before we get into developing a continuous learning mindset, let us take a look at a simple and intuitive way to classify the learning we undergo and contrast it with the learning that AI agents undergo:

The chart we are looking at here simplifies how human learning works. It has been broken down into two key aspects: one, the balance between being active and passive in the learning process, and two, whether there's a teacher or mentor present during the learning journey. These two aspects combine to create four types of learning experiences.

As kids, our primary mode of learning is rather passive, and we usually have teachers or parents guiding us through this phase. In the world of artificial intelligence, this resembles supervised learning. Think of early AI algorithms being trained by humans – it is a bit like having a teacher or mentor instructing AI systems.

But as we grow older and start navigating the world on our own, a significant portion of our learning becomes more active

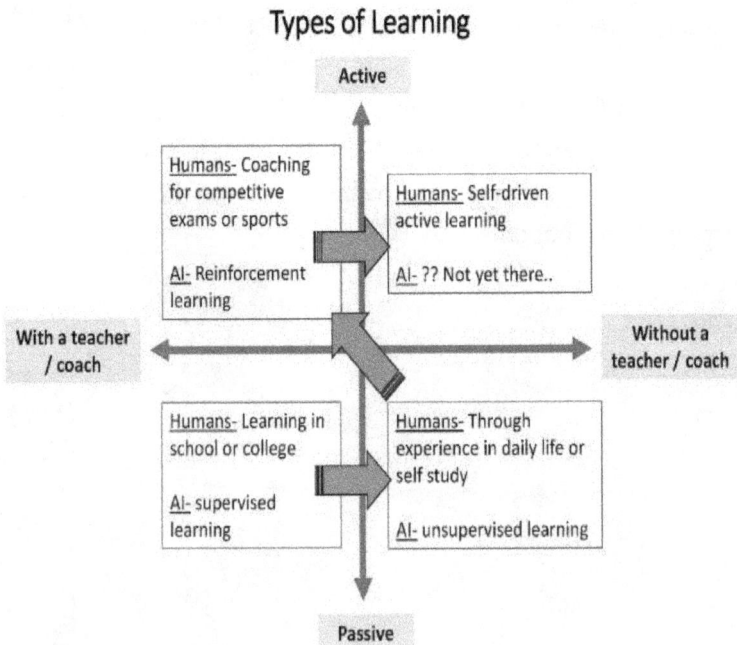

Types of Learning

Active

| Humans- Coaching for competitive exams or sports

AI- Reinforcement learning | Humans- Self-driven active learning

AI- ?? Not yet there.. |

With a teacher / coach ←——————→ **Without a teacher / coach**

| Humans- Learning in school or college

AI- supervised learning | Humans- Through experience in daily life or self study

AI- unsupervised learning |

Passive

and less teacher-dependent. This stage coincides with our working years when we learn by doing and observing. In AI terms, this kind of learning is referred to as unsupervised learning, where AI systems sift through vast datasets to identify patterns and make sense of things.

Now, here is where things get intriguing. Most of us occasionally engage in learning through coaching, especially if we're professional athletes or preparing for a competitive exam. Coaching plays a pivotal role in refining skills and knowledge. Many modern AI advancements fall under this category, which is known as reinforcement learning in AI lingo.

The fourth and most advanced level of learning is something we rarely think about. It is self-driven active learning, where we delve into learning purely out of curiosity and to quench our thirst for knowledge. We mentioned Leonardo da Vinci's To-Do list earlier – that's a perfect example of someone pushing themselves to explore various subjects for the sheer joy of learning. AI has not yet reached this stage because it requires intrinsic motivation and curiosity to drive self-learning. Today's AI systems lack the self-awareness or volition needed for self-driven exploration. This unique ability is, for now, exclusive to humans.

In a world that is moving more nonlinearly and rapidly, focusing on the first two stages of learning (supervised and unsupervised) may not be enough. To thrive in this dynamic environment, it's crucial to cultivate the latter two stages of learning. And given how quickly things change in this nonlinear world, it demands a continuous learning mindset – the willingness to keep adapting and growing.

However, this is a long journey. To support a continuous learning mindset, let us delve into the Shu Ha Ri framework— Shu Ha Ri originates from the Japanese martial art Aikido and describes the stages of learning to mastery. The term Shu ha ri roughly translates to "first learn, then detach, and finally transcend." Aikido master Endō Seishirō Shihan explains the idea as follows: *"It is known that, when we learn or train in something, we pass through the stages of Shu, Ha, and Ri. These stages are explained as follows. In Shu, we repeat the forms and discipline ourselves so that our bodies absorb the forms that our forebears created. We remain faithful to these forms with no deviation. Next, in the stage of Ha, once we have disciplined ourselves to acquire the forms and movements, we make innovations. In this process, the forms may be broken and discarded. Finally, in Ri, we completely depart from the forms, open the door to creative technique, and arrive in a place where we act following what our heart/mind desires, unhindered while not overstepping laws."*

With the passage of time, the martial arts concept of Shu Ha Ri has been abstracted and applied to the cycle of learning. Agile thinkers like Martin Fowler and Alistair Cockburn have written about using and applying Shu Ha Ri in agile environments. Martin Fowler applied the Shu Ha Ri framework to learning as follows: The beginning stage is Shu, where the student follows the teachings and instructions of their master. He focuses on performing the task without contemplating too much about the underlying theory. The second stage, Ha, is the point when the disciple tries to branch out. With basic knowledge and understanding, he learns the underlying principles and theory behind the abovementioned technique. In this stage, he implements his learnings into practice. Finally, in the last step, Ra, the student learns entirely from his own practice and not from other individuals. He builds his framework and approaches and adapts what he has learned over time. This learning needs to happen outside the formal education system. By acquiring the Shu Ha Ri mindset, one can learn new skills and sharpen them for better purposes.

Thus, in this chapter, we have learned that to keep up with the nonlinear world and maximize its benefits, we need to adopt reskilling as our default mindset. Some of the changes are inevitable. How we adapt to them is the right question to ask. In the era of nonlinearity; uncertainty and change are given. Thus, inculcating a curious and continuously adapting mindset can ease ambiguity by focusing on the positives of learning, improving, and overall development. Re-skilling needs to be seen as a continuous journey & the Shu-Ha-Ri framework can provide guidance on adopting a continuous learning mindset. Everything we discussed in this chapter boils down to the perfect quote written by Idowu Koyenikan, *"The mind is just like a muscle - the more you exercise it, the stronger it gets and the more it can expand."*

CONCLUSION

As we approach the conclusion of this book, we have delved into the intricacies of our nonlinear world and how things were in the linear era. Back then, access to information and communication was far more limited than our current reality, where a wealth of knowledge is just a click away. It is an exciting time, and I hope you share my enthusiasm for the Digital Renaissance, which is revolutionizing traditional creative fields. This transformative period introduces a concept called "HumAInism," where humans and Artificial Intelligence combine their strengths for remarkable advancements. However, while we stand on the cusp of this thrilling journey, we must tread carefully and prepare ourselves adequately. The content of this book is meant to equip you for this upcoming expedition.

In the introduction, we traced the path of human interaction with technology through the three epochs, always considering that the fourth epoch is on the horizon. Our world has undergone a rapid transformation thanks to technological evolution. Life was quite different before modern technology became integral to our existence. Today, our smartphones, electronic devices, medical breakthroughs, industrial innovations, transportation systems, and more have profoundly simplified our lives.

This technological convenience and efficiency have led to significant improvements in our daily lives. It's remarkable to consider that not too long ago, even basic tasks like doing laundry could consume an entire day. The shift in our way of life has been nothing short of remarkable.

In contrast, today, we have washing machines to relieve us of the burdensome task of laundry. Technology has opened up countless opportunities that hold a significant place in our lives. Unlike past technologies, present-day technology has the unique capability of reducing and increasing our mental load. This duality arises from the growing nonlinearity that characterizes our contemporary world.

While modern technology can alleviate some of our mental burdens by automating and simplifying certain tasks, it also introduces new complexities and information overload due to today's highly interconnected and nonlinear world. Our relationship with technology is multifaceted, and its impact on our mental load reflects the intricate interplay between convenience and the challenges posed by our dynamic and ever-evolving digital landscape.

Technology Through Epochs

	Epoch 1	Epoch 2	Epoch 3	Epoch 4
Time period	Hunter-gatherer days of our ancestors before agriculture and permanent settlements came into being (from 3 Mn years BC till 2500 BC)	From 2500 BC till middle of 20th century	From middle of 20th century till now	The increasingly nonlinear future leading to Digital Renaissance!
Primary role of technology	To make lives safe	Harnessing natural resources – readily available or processed – mainly to save physical efforts	Faster computation, data storage and transfer to drive digitalization and mass customization	Technology as co-pilot for humans 24 X 7
Examples of key technologies	Stone / bronze / iron tools for better hunting and protection	Domesticated animals for farming, water / steam power, electricity, internal combustion engines using fossil fuel, nuclear power	Computers, smartphones, internet, machine learning algorithms, social media	Generative AI, nanotechnology in healthcare, quantum computing
Impact on people	Less physical efforts to hunt, more physical safety	Less physical efforts, better quality of living, better physical connectivity	Better productivity, reducing mental load. At the same time increasing mental load	Do we have the DeSiRe to face the nonlinear world and usher in Digital Renaissance

In Chapter 1, we examined how our world thrives on nonlinearity, how it is dynamic, and how we no longer follow a set pattern of rules and make our own preferred choices instead. In the next chapter, we delved into the impact of nonlinearity on our minds and our attention spans. Even though technology has shaped our lives in several ways, we face many disadvantages, too. If we are not careful, we risk our brains getting rewired under pressure from all the nonlinearity.

Undoubtedly, technology is often being used imprudently, leading to complexity. In the third chapter, we examined how Artificial Intelligence could fasten the positive and negative impact in the nonlinear world. In Chapter 4, we witnessed how Artificial Intelligence has the potential to usher in the Digital Renaissance. We looked back at many centuries into the Classical Renaissance for inspiration and to establish parallels. Chapters 1-4 underlined the need for us to be prepared to make the most of the upcoming Digital Renaissance.

Chapters 5-8 focus more on my "DeSIRe framework' as a guide to thriving in a nonlinear world. Delinking and Simplifying are good starting points to be prepared. Investing and reskilling stages offer a few handy suggestions for adapting to the nonlinearity.

As we wrap up this book, take a moment to contemplate the swift changes unfolding around us. Nonlinearity can be overwhelming, but with a strong desire to excel and my DeSIRe framework as your guide, you can illuminate your path forward. Embrace your humanity—conquer challenges, adapt, and progress. Your nonlinear world awaits. I wish you all the best in your journey towards the Digital Renaissance!

AN AFTERTHOUGHT

If you have a managerial, teaching or parenting role and are responsible for grooming adults or children, here's something you should know:

This book was written keeping in mind an individual reader. But many of us have managerial roles where we are responsible for grooming, coaching and mentoring our reportees or subordinates. Some of us are in a teaching profession where we have the noble task of shaping the minds of children or youth. And needless to say, many of us have parental responsibilities that involve shaping a bright future for our children or wards. What should the subject matter of this book mean to such people? Well, the entire contents of this book are equally relevant for teachers and students, managers and employees, parents and children. After all, technology has impacted and will continue to impact everyone.

However, if you happen to play the role of a manager, teacher or parent, I would suggest an addendum to the DeSIRe framework. I call this E^3 framework.

E^3 Framework

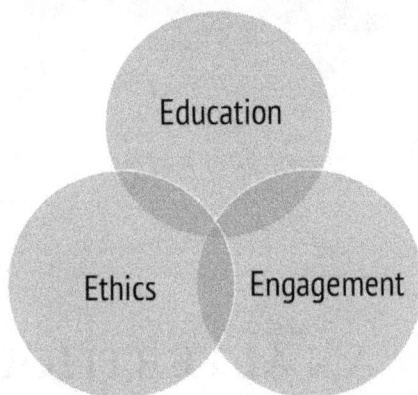

Let's look at the three 'E' in detail:

Education

Earlier, we differentiated between knowledge and skills. We also identified creative, collaborative and curative skills as being critical to making the most out of the Digital Renaissance that awaits us round the corner. We examined the role of diagnostic reasoning as well. Alas, our education system is not geared to address the challenges arising out of our nonlinear world. Our education system values learning by rote and doesn't encourage diversity of opinion and creativity. As a manager, teacher or parent, wouldn't it be wonderful if you are able to supplement the formal education by inculcating diagnostic reasoning and skills based learning in those in your care?

Ethics

Earlier we saw that the confluence of human + AI (or HumAInism) will be a cornerstone of Digital Renaissance. However, this will also throw up interesting ethical conundrums. Where does the human accountability start and stop when a human is being co-piloted by AI (take self-driving cars as an example)? Where does the human capability start and stop when a human is taking help from Generative AI? Who carries the burden if an AI system fails- the one who provided the data to train AI algorithms or the one who developed the AI algorithm or the one who marketed the AI solution? Will Generative AI lead to interesting intellectual property of copyright issues? All of these are valid questions, but we do not know the valid answers. Proliferation of AI will lead to many more such ethical and moral dilemmas. As managers, teachers and parents, our effort should be to instil a strong sense of morality and ethics in those in our care, while encouraging AI usage.

Engagement

As the third epoch of technology usage started with the internet and even before the advent of AI, digital technology has indeed started affecting our brains. Earlier, we discussed some of the perils of excessive technology usage in today's nonlinear world. Lowering of attention spans, the doer role taking precedence over the planner role are just some of these perils. As the Digital Renaissance is ushered in, there is a grave danger of people spending more time with technology rather than with fellow humans. This will be most unfortunate. In-person connection and a sense of community has always been a bedrock of Humanity. Asocial and sometimes anti-social behaviour due to excessive technology usage could prove detrimental to this camaraderie. As John Donne eloquently described- No man is an island entire of itself. Our destinies are inter-twined and we have always progressed as humanity. As managers, parents and teachers, it is up to us to encourage this strong sense of connectedness amongst each other.

I am sure that by not only following the DeSIRe framework, but also by following the E^3 tenets, we could help those in our care to embrace the Digital Renaissance with positivity and confidence.

www.ingramcontent.com/pod-product-compliance
Lightning Source LLC
Chambersburg PA
CBHW031516040426
42445CB00009B/254